for **Supporting Education**

**Eileen Fursland with
Kate Cairns and Chris Stanway**

BAAF
ADOPTION
& FOSTERING

Published by
**British Association for Adoption & Fostering
(BAAF)**
Saffron House
6–10 Kirby Street
London EC1N 8TS
www.baaf.org.uk

Charity registration 275689 (England and Wales)
and SC039337 (Scotland)

British Library Cataloguing in Publication Data
A catalogue record for this book is available from the British Library

ISBN 978 1 907585 71 5

Project management by Jo Francis, Publications Department, BAAF
Designed by Helen Joubert Designs
Typeset by Fravashi Aga
Printed in Great Britain by T J International Ltd

Trade distribution by Turnaround Publisher Services, Unit 3,
Olympia Trading Estate, Coburg Road, London N22 6TZ

BAAF is the leading UK-wide membership organisation for all those
concerned with adoption, fostering and child care issues.

Contents

This series

Ten Top Tips for Supporting Education is the eleventh title in BAAF's *Ten Top Tips* series. This series tackles some fundamental issues in the area of adoption and fostering with the aim of presenting them in a quick reference format. Previous titles are:

- *Ten Top Tips for Placing Children*, by Hedi Argent
- *Ten Top Tips for Managing Contact*, by Henrietta Bond
- *Ten Top Tips for Finding Families*, by Jennifer Cousins
- *Ten Top Tips for Placing Siblings*, by Hedi Argent
- *Ten Top Tips for Preparing Care Leavers*, by Henrietta Bond
- *Ten Top Tips for Making Introductions*, by Lindsey Dunbar
- *Ten Top Tips for Supporting Kinship Placements*, by Hedi Argent
- *Ten Top Tips for Supporting Adopters*, by Jeanne Kaniuk with Eileen Fursland
- *Ten Top Tips for Identifying Neglect*, by Pat Beesley
- *Ten Top Tips for Making Matches*, by Jennifer Cousins

Details are available on www.baaf.org.uk.

Acknowledgements

Heartfelt thanks to Kate Cairns and Chris Stanway for so generously sharing with me their extensive knowledge and experience of supporting the education of children who have suffered trauma and adversity. I am also grateful to Shaila Shah and Jo Francis at BAAF for bringing this book to publication.

Notes about the authors

Eileen Fursland is a freelance writer. She has written extensively for BAAF as well as for a range of magazines and national newspapers. Eileen's publications for BAAF include her books *Facing up to Facebook*; *Social Networking and Contact*; *Foster Care and Social Networking*; and a booklet for young people, *Social Networking and You*. In previous collaborations with Kate Cairns, she co-wrote BAAF's training programmes: *Trauma and Recovery*; *Safer Caring*; *Building Identity*; and *Transitions and Endings*.

Eileen designs and delivers training sessions for local authorities and other organisations around the UK, to help foster carers, adopters and social workers to meet the challenges posed by social networking. She has also led workshops for foster carers and practitioners as part of Cambridge University's Realise project, which aims to raise educational aspirations among looked after young people.

Kate Cairns is an author, speaker and trainer with an international reputation for her work around attachment, trauma and resilience, particularly in relation to vulnerable children and young people. She has authored several books for BAAF, including *Attachment, Trauma and Resilience* (2002). She has been a social worker for 40 years, and a trainer for 20 years. With her husband Brian and their three birth children, Kate provided a permanent family for 12 other children between 1975 and 1997. In 2004, Kate founded Akamas Ltd, which developed pioneering online qualifications for foster care and the broader children's workforce, before it became part of the ALS group in 2009.

Chris Stanway worked for 32 years in a state secondary school in an area with high levels of social deprivation. Having progressed through a number of roles within the school, including SENCO, she established the role of Designated Teacher for Looked After Children. As an Assistant Headteacher, she established and ran an inclusion unit within the mainstream school. Together with Kate Cairns, she wrote *Learn the Child: Helping looked after children to learn* (BAAF, 2004, 2nd edition 2013). She now works as an independent consultant producing materials specifically focused for the education workforce. Finding positive ways of working with children who find life and learning in school difficult remains Chris' prime motivator.

Introduction

Doing well at school can make a huge difference to a child's life chances. Like a stable, caring foster placement, education can help to redress some of the damage and disadvantage that affect the lives of children in care. When things go well, school can provide a looked after child with stability, security and a good education, which can be the key to a happier, more fulfilled and more successful future.

By supporting a looked after child to thrive in school, in partnership with foster carers and other professionals, you can make a positive difference to her life. The aim of this book is to suggest some of the ways you can work with the child, the school and other people around her to help her to reach her potential at school and beyond.

Education is a large subject and this book – intentionally – is a fairly short, succinct guide. As such, it cannot cover every aspect of this topic. However, by concentrating on ten top tips for supporting children in education, it provides a solid starting point, with ideas suggested for ways to continue engaging with this subject.

It should also be noted that this book refers to the education system in England. However, although the system and the terminology used in Wales, Scotland and Northern Ireland do differ, the suggestions and practical advice in this guide for supporting children's education are generally applicable UK-wide.

Some children and young people enjoy their school life and achieve great results. But we know that, on average, children and young people in the care system do not do as well at school as their peers.[1]

- Of children continuously looked after for 12 months during the year to 31 March 2012, just 15.5 per cent achieved GCSEs graded A* to C in English and mathematics at Key Stage 4, compared with 58.7 per cent of children who were not looked after.

- The attainment gap starts to show early on in many of these children's school careers. In 2012, according to Key Stage 1 teacher assessments (at age seven), 67 per cent of looked after children achieved the expected level in reading (compared with 87 per cent of non-looked after children); 57 per cent of looked after children achieved the expected level in writing (compared with 83 per cent of non-looked after children); and 71 per cent in maths (compared with 91 per cent of non-looked after children).

- The disparity is evident at age 11 in Key Stage 2 tests, where 50 per cent of looked after children achieved level 4 or above in both English and maths, compared with 79 per cent of non-looked after children.

- Looked after children and young people are four times more likely to be permanently excluded from school than their peers (in England, 0.3 per cent were permanently excluded in 2010–11, compared with 0.07 per cent of all children).

Why should this be the case? There are many reasons. A chaotic home life, neglect and abuse in the first few years of life cause trauma and affect the developing brain, leading to a range of difficulties with emotions, behaviour, learning, memory and relating to other children and adults. All of this makes functioning in school more of a challenge. Many children experience a lack of stability even after they are removed from their inadequate, neglectful or abusive families and taken into care. After being uprooted once and placed in a new and alien environment, some go on to experience further moves, perhaps moving from one foster home to another or even back home and then

---

[1] Information on looked after children is published by the Department for Education as part of the *Statistical First Release, Outcomes for children looked after by local authorities in England, as at 31 March 2012*. This can be found at: www.education.gov.uk/rsgateway/DB/SFR/s001103/sfr32-2012v2.pdf.

possibly returning to care later. Stress takes over for the child. Learning takes a back seat. How can you learn when you are overwhelmed with anxiety? How can you see the point of working hard at school when you hold out no hope for the future? Many children in care have experienced periods out of school, making them fall behind their peers. If a placement or change of placement also involves a change of school, children may fall even further behind and struggle to catch up, or perhaps give up trying.

However, it is not inevitable that children and young people in the care system will fail to achieve educationally. Some do well, in spite of all the challenges facing them.

In the year 2000, Mohammad Razai arrived in Dover aged 15, accompanied by his younger cousin. In Mohammad's early childhood his father had been executed by the then Communist government in Afghanistan. Mohammad and his family belonged to the persecuted minority of the Shia Hazara ethnic group, and when the Taliban took over Kabul their life became more dangerous than ever. An uncle was murdered in prison. Mohammad's mother arranged for him to escape from Afghanistan and the threat of the Taliban. It was a frightening journey into the unknown for the 15-year-old.

When he arrived in the UK, he spoke almost no English. He was placed in foster care first in Kent and then in London, where an "amazing" and "life-transforming" social worker (Mohammad's own words) entered his young life and arranged for him to go to school:

> *She called people and was really, really pushy.*
> *She would say: 'No, this is not good enough'.[2]*

After settling into education, he completed his GCSEs in an intensive, single year, followed by A-levels, and went on to study anatomy and developmental biology at University College, London. Then he was accepted to study medicine at Cambridge University. Now Mohammad is about to graduate from Cambridge with a medical degree. He is a British citizen and his eventual dream is to become a paediatrician:

> *I really want to do something useful, to do some good in the world.[2]*

Of course, not all children and young people in care will be able to reach these academic heights, but we need to ensure that they can all reach their full potential, whatever that may be.

> *Local authorities have a duty to safeguard and to promote the welfare of the children they look after. They also have a particular duty to promote the educational achievement of the children they look after, regardless of where they live.*
>
> *This means that local authorities must consider the educational implications of every decision taken about a child's care placement. This reflects their wider role as a corporate parent – local authorities must strive to offer all the support that a good parent would give in order to make sure that the children they look after reach their full potential.*
>
> *(Department for Education, 2012c)*

There is a volume of statutory guidance called *Promoting the Educational Achievement of Looked After Children: Statutory guidance for local authorities* (Department for Children, Schools and Families, 2010a) to help local authorities to implement their statutory duty.

Most children and young people who are not in the care system have the love and care of parents who really want them to do well in school, who help and encourage them all they can and who, if necessary, will fight tooth and nail to find them the support they need

---

[2] 'Mohammad Razai: from child Afghan asylum seeker to Cambridge undergraduate', Kate Kellaway, *The Observer*, 20.6.10

or to get them a place in the best school in their area. What most children in care need is someone who will fight their corner with the same commitment and passion. How can "corporate parents", in the shape of the local authority, social workers, foster carers and teachers, become more like these parents? How can they advocate for the child as effectively as those "pushy", sharp-elbowed parents who are determined to do whatever it takes to ensure that their child does well at school? If you have that same determination, we hope this book will help you to use it to achieve the very best for the children and young people in your care.

TIP 1

Learn the child

What is the child's own narrative about himself and about education?

> *...most powerful of all are the stories nobody hears. The stories we tell inside our own heads, attempting to make sense of the world and of our place within it. Seldom consciously articulated, they nonetheless have the profoundest effect on how we feel about our lives and even on how we live them.*
>
> *(Allan, 2012)*

Narratives are formed early in life. The story or internal narrative which children form about themselves and their lives is shaped by their early experiences and the messages they have been given – directly or indirectly – by the adults around them. The child may never have seen his parents open a book. His parents may never bother to wake him up in time for school. They may have told him things like: 'I hated school'; 'You're stupid'; or 'You'll never be any good at anything'. These messages can influence the child's view of himself so that he sees himself as destined to fail at school. The child's narrative may also involve opposition to education, for instance, if he is told: 'Teachers are idiots' and 'School is a waste of time'.

Many looked after children have experienced neglect and trauma (see below). These experiences in early life can have a profound effect on a child's ability to learn and function in school. A vicious circle can develop, in which the child's behaviour and learning difficulties lead to his receiving negative messages about himself from teachers and his peers, reinforcing his negative internal narrative. Even if he sometimes does something well and is praised, this negative narrative can be so overwhelming that he almost literally can't hear the positive message and therefore disregards it.

Foster carers, teachers and others who are working with the child need to be aware of the wide-ranging impact of neglect, abuse and trauma, and of the child's own narrative about education. This will give them a deeper understanding of why he behaves as he does and how they can help him.

Narratives are resistant to change. It takes time and effort, and the people who work with and teach the child need to take on this task if he is to be able to take full advantage of opportunities to learn and achieve in school.

What are the child's perceived strengths and difficulties?

Unlike most other children, looked after children have lived through difficult and traumatic events and experiences and their lives have been marked by disruption and loss. In spite of this, many of these children somehow manage to be as cheerful, funny, delightful, creative, kind, curious and keen to learn as other children. We should recognise and celebrate their strengths.

If a child is doing well at subjects such as English and maths, that is a strength. But not all children will shine academically. Don't underestimate the importance of the child's out-of-school skills, activities and interests.

When a child or young person is struggling in lessons and is in danger of becoming demotivated in school, we need to find his other strengths and use these constructively to help him engage with the school. For example, if he is good at football or athletics, if he's a whizz on the computer, if he is learning to play the guitar, the teachers can look for opportunities to use these skills and interests in school, which will give him a "reason" to go to school and encourage him to feel more positive about it.

Many children in care have emotional, mental and physical health needs that impact on their education. For example, some are struggling with the legacy of neglect and abuse, instability and disruption in their early life. Some have conditions such as foetal alcohol spectrum disorder (FASD), attention deficit hyperactivity disorder (ADHD), learning difficulties and autism spectrum disorders (ASD).

When thinking about how best to support a looked after child at school, we need to consider his strengths and difficulties in global terms, not just in terms of education. Educational attainment is strongly linked to the child's social, emotional and behavioural development.

The legacy of childhood neglect and trauma

If a baby's attachment needs are not met, if he does not have a carer who is reliable and attuned to him and he does not develop a sense of safety, he will not develop the ability to regulate stress and his brain function will be compromised. This is **developmental trauma**.

Some children develop the ability to regulate stress in babyhood but then, at a stage when they are able to process their feelings, they are exposed to terrifying events. They may be threatened or fear for their lives, or see someone close to them threatened or beaten, for example. Overwhelming fear or horror leads to extreme stress and the brain floods the body with massive amounts of stress hormones. These cause major areas of brain function to close down, while other areas become activated and sensitised. This is **emotional trauma**.

If the child cannot recover spontaneously from either developmental or emotional trauma, these changes of function persist and he develops symptoms of post-traumatic stress disorder.

For children, separation from their primary attachment figure – even if that person is a source of harm – represents a threat.

Childhood trauma can have a long-term or permanent damaging effect on cognitive functions such as learning and memory, on all major body systems, and on emotional and social functioning. In time, the child will adapt to his impairments. But adapting can lead to behaviours and other symptoms of disorder that can be puzzling to other people. Every aspect of his life is likely to be affected – including his behaviour, how he manages his emotions, his ability to learn and his ability to understand, empathise with and interact with other people and to form attachments.

Hyperarousal

Physiologically, the inner state of traumatised people is one of terror. The traumatised child is in a perpetual state of stress and in some cases the child adapts to accommodate this highly aroused state as his "normality". Some children remain hyperaroused and behave accordingly, for example, finding it impossible to relax or sit quietly and becoming addicted to high-stimulus activities such as computer games or creating tension in people around them. The child may always be "hypervigilant" or on the alert for danger, and will perceive neutral stimuli as threatening. Attention and concentration are both severely reduced by hypervigilance, which obviously makes learning difficult.

Dissociation

Some children "dissociate" in response to their physiological state of high stress arousal. Humans have the ability to filter out certain parts of our experience to prevent us from being overwhelmed by stimuli. In dissociation, as a survival mechanism in the face of an overwhelming threat, the child splits his awareness so that he becomes cut off from his own experiences and emotions, as though behind a glass wall. His distress may be less apparent than that of hyperaroused children, but it causes him harm nonetheless.

Some children alternate between hyperarousal and dissociation. Some children experience physiological and physical effects such as altered vision and hearing; altered sleep and eating patterns; headaches, digestive disorders, muscle tension and other psychosomatic illnesses; and compulsive self-harm.

Avoidance

For a traumatised child, certain things will trigger memories of the trauma. This may be, for example, a particular smell or activity, or a certain place or person. The child who has not recovered from trauma will not be able to distinguish realistic triggers from neutral stimuli and may show avoidant behaviour, avoiding certain aspects of daily life without having any understanding of the reasons for his own behaviour.

How post-traumatic stress disorder can affect the child's school life

Children with post-traumatic stress disorders find it hard to make sense of the world. Without someone to help them recover and explain to them how trauma has affected them, they do not understand why they behave and feel the way they do. Their behaviour may be both disturbed and disturbing, and can lead to their constantly getting into trouble.

- They may be unpredictable and prone to antisocial behaviour, aggression, self-harm or extreme reactions of panic or anger – which can make other children wary or frightened of them.

- They may struggle to understand the idea of ownership and the difference between "mine" and "yours", so they take other people's possessions and get in trouble for stealing.

- Many traumatised children have difficulty developing empathy with others. This, along with their often "odd" behaviour and unpredictability, can lead to them becoming socially isolated and often lonely. Some gravitate towards other damaged children and become members of a deviant peer group in which they gain acceptance and even credit for defiant and destructive behaviour inside and outside school.

- If some person, place or activity in school triggers memories of abuse (e.g. the appearance, voice or smell of a particular teacher or classroom in school might bring to mind the person who abused the child, or having a shower after a games lesson might trigger memories of abuse that took place in a shower), the child may take avoiding action, such as, say, walking out of the classroom or failing to turn up to a lesson. If the reason for such behaviour is not understood, it is likely to land him in trouble.

Consider these scenarios, which illustrate how a traumatised child might behave in the classroom and why his teachers may sometimes misunderstand and use mistaken behaviour modification strategies to cope with the behaviour.

● The teacher asks the child: 'Why did you do that?' The child – dissociated from his feelings and emotions – genuinely has no idea and no words to describe his feelings, so he simply shrugs.

● The teacher says to the child: 'Look at me when I'm talking to you'. The hyperaroused child avoids eye contact because he finds it so intensely stimulating that it's almost physically impossible for him to comply. To the teacher, it appears that the child is simply being defiant.

● The child's classmates laugh at him for saying something silly. Unable to cope with his overwhelming feeling of shame and humiliation, and with a diminished capacity for impulse control, he lashes out and throws a chair. The teacher can't understand why this child reacts so strongly to a "minor" provocation.

● The child who was abused as a toddler has become obsessed with stories involving violence and horror, and in the classroom he is constantly referring to people being hurt and killed. Traumatic stress has taken over his core identity. The teacher finds it hard to know how to deal with his preoccupation, which is disturbing some of the other children.

In all these cases, what the child needs is help to recover from and adapt to the effects of overwhelming post-traumatic stress. How can we do this? For more information, read work by Kate Cairns and others on trauma and recovery and how to help traumatised children to stabilise, integrate, adapt and gain self-esteem, a sense of social connectedness and the capacity for joy (Cairns and Fursland, 2007; Cairns and Stanway, 2010).

When a strength can become a difficulty

In some cases, a single quality or attribute in the child can present as either a strength or a difficulty, or both. For example:

● A child may be a good leader and able to influence his peers, which is a strength. However, in some contexts it can become a difficulty. If a child who is a good leader is in opposition to the school, he may be, or be perceived to be, a ringleader for bad behaviour.

● A child affected by foetal alcohol spectrum disorder may typically be very outgoing and keen to engage with others and please the teacher – yet his lack of awareness of social cues and conventions may lead to his being rejected by peers and perceived as attention-seeking by the teacher. If no positive attention is forthcoming, then he may do whatever it takes to get extra attention, even if this is negative attention.

● A child with Asperger's Syndrome or an autism spectrum disorder may be very bright and have a formidable capacity for concentrating on and researching in depth a subject that interests him. However, he may focus on this one interest to the exclusion of everything else.

● A child who is intelligent and highly motivated to learn and work hard in school may be singled out, ridiculed or even bullied by his peers who are less able and have different values.

● A child who is much more able than his peers may be unstimulated by the lessons and, to relieve his boredom, become disruptive in class.

Screening tools and rating scales

Has a "**Strengths and Difficulties Questionnaire**" been completed for this child by anyone in the network of professionals around him? The Strengths and Difficulties Questionnaire (SDQ) is a screening tool which can be used to identify emotional or behavioural problems. The full SDQ consists of a questionnaire for the carers, one for the child and one for the teacher. For more information, visit www.sdqscore.org and www.youthinmind.info/.

If this has not been done by the school or any other agency, you may need to initiate an SDQ and have the results interpreted by an educational psychologist or a psychologist from the child and adolescent mental health service (CAMHS). The most effective way to get the SDQ done may be to initiate it during a care or education planning meeting, when considering future actions that are needed for the child.

With the completed SDQ, interpreted by an expert, you will have a fuller understanding of the child's strengths and difficulties. This, along with your role as corporate parent for this child, will enable you to work more effectively with the school.

Another assessment tool sometimes used on a whole-school or small group basis is the "**Pupil Attitudes to Self and School**" (PASS) questionnaire, which looks at pupils' motivations and concerns, such as their sense of belonging to the school and their confidence. Regardless of the children's attainment levels, a high PASS score among its pupils can assure a school that it is doing a good job in terms of how positively children feel about the school. Looking at the results for an individual child may throw light on the child's attitudes to school.

What are the key issues in terms of vulnerability and resilience for this child?

Resilience is the ability to adapt, survive and thrive in difficult conditions. Resilient people continue to develop and reach their potential even when circumstances are against them. This is different from merely coping, when people survive adversity but in the process their development is impaired in some way. We are all resilient and vulnerable at the same time, and our resilience and vulnerability are changing all the time in response to circumstances and events.

Children can be helped to adapt and increase their resilience, whatever difficulties they have survived. Factors increasing resilience in vulnerable children can be categorised into six domains (Daniel and Wassell, 2002):

- Secure base
- Education

- Friendships

- Talents and interests

- Positive values

- Social competencies

Having a secure base is the foundation on which all the other domains depend. The lack of a sense of permanence can make a child less resilient. Looked after children and young people are likely to lack a sense of permanence because of uncertainty about the future plans for them. Some have no idea whether they will be returning home, staying in the placement or being moved to another placement, or what will happen when they leave care.

Some children may be resilient in some areas of their lives, but struggle in others. They may have a sense of security in the foster placement and a stable attachment relationship with the carers, but struggle with school life or friendships, for example. For other children, going to school is the most stable element in an otherwise insecure life.

Out-of-school interests and activities can contribute powerfully to resilience, particularly for children and young people who have had few opportunities to develop motivation and experience success in the classroom:

> *A leisure interest may provide their first real experience of being motivated – a critical factor in achievement. For young people who have often had broken schooling, study support/out-of-school-hours learning activities can be a route back into formal learning and achievement. Gains in self-confidence, and the chance to build relationships, can provide much-needed stability – of care and school placements.*
>
> *(ContinYou, 2005)*

Some children may appear outwardly to be coping, and because they are not overtly disturbed or showing signs of being troubled, people around them may assume they are fine and say things like: 'They are very resilient'. But in many cases this is simply not true. Many looked after children have not had the opportunity to develop attachments, or have had disrupted attachments, and this has diminished their social resilience. Without social resilience, children cannot do well at school.

Looked after young people have poorer mental health than their peers

The mental health and emotional well-being of looked after children and young people is known to be much poorer than their peers in the general population. The most extensive study of the mental health of looked after children and young people (Melzer et al, 2002) found that among 11- to 15-year-olds who were looked after, 55 per cent of boys and 43 per cent of girls had a mental health disorder. A study of looked after children and young people who had been in care for at least a year reviewed their case files at their point of entry into care and identified that at that point, 72 per cent of looked after children aged between 5 and 15 had a mental or behavioural problem (Sempik et al, 2008).

(Ryan, 2012)

Even among looked after children and young people who have not been diagnosed with a mental health disorder, there will be many who still seem somehow different from their peers – perhaps more withdrawn, less confident, less able to make and keep friends, more easily distracted, easily upset or quick to "blow up" when teased or thwarted.

15

Emotional and social well-being and educational outcomes

There is new evidence that emotional and social well-being is linked to academic achievement. A recent report for the Department for Education by researchers at the Childhood Wellbeing Research Centre (Gutman and Vorhaus, 2012) investigates the association between dimensions of well-being at ages seven to 13 and concurrent (i.e. measured at the same age) and later educational outcomes at ages 11 to 16, including academic achievement (i.e. national exam scores) and school engagement (i.e. being stimulated by school). Among the findings were:

● 'Children with **higher levels of emotional, behavioural, social, and school well-being**, on average, have higher levels of academic achievement and are more engaged in school, both concurrently and in later years.

● Children with **better emotional well-being** make more progress in primary school and are more engaged in secondary school.'

An important part of the social worker's role is to assess the child's vulnerability and resilience, and to see how it might be possible to build up his resilience.

Consider the people around the child

Each child is embedded in a network of other people. Adults who understand the attachment process and the effects of unmet attachment needs and trauma are equipped to help the child develop resilience. Some of these people will be an actual or potential source of strength for the child, so we need to look at the child in the centre of his network rather than in isolation.

Consider the people around the child – everyone in the foster family, the wider birth family, the school and any local community groups the child and family belong to, such as Scouts, football club, and so on. Who could potentially build up his resilience, and can you help them to see how they could do this?

Listen to the child

Listen to the child and find out what the big issues are for him. Ask him what, if anything, is difficult for him about school.

When I was in school I found it very difficult to make new friends, and to fit in. This was due to being in foster care and moving schools a lot. When starting a new school I always had to make the teachers aware I was in foster care, just in case I had an appointment with my social worker during school time. Having these appointments during school time was the hardest, they made me different, and no one else had to leave the class for an hour or so. Then there were always the questions afterwards, 'What's so special about her that she gets to skip a lesson?'

Other issues include everyday life such as holidays (Mother's Day, Father's Day, Christmas). I felt like no one understood why it was so hard for me to sit down and make a card 'for the best mother in the world'. This impacted on my life, I was being bullied for getting special treatment from teachers and losing friends because they didn't understand. Feeling isolated and alone is the worst feeling in the world; even though being in school with over 200 people, I was still alone.

(Naina Thomas, in foreword to In Care In School *(Bath Spa University and Bath and North East Somerset Council, 2012))*

What help does the child need from you?

As the child's social worker, you too can of course be a source of strength for him. In 2006, the Office of the Children's Rights Director in England asked children and young people their views about social workers – some of the results are given below.

Type of help young people wanted from their social workers

- Help with personal problems

- To be listened to

- Help to stay safe

- Help with getting ready to leave care

By providing children and young people with question cards to fill in, the researchers asked what **other areas** they needed help with at the moment, but were not getting help with, on top of those they had suggested. They received 91 answers listing additional sorts of help children and young people said they needed, but were not getting, from social workers. Top of the list was **help with education**, including practical things like equipment and uniforms, as well as **help with schoolwork** (16 children and young people said this).

The Office of the Children's Rights Director also consulted with children and young people in discussion groups:

*Some told us of things they needed their social workers to arrange for them…other things we heard about in our groups included getting hold of **computers** that were needed for school or college work – and getting these at the time you needed them. When social workers managed this, they were praised by the young person they had helped in this sort of way. **Getting you into a suitable school** was also something some children and young people told us they wanted their social workers to do for them.*

(Office of the Children's Rights Director for England, 2006)

Look for hidden talents and encourage out-of-school interests

Something really valuable that you can do for the young person in your care is to help them work out what they enjoy doing and encourage them (and the foster carers) to consider out-of-school and holiday activities and clubs or groups. As well as sheer pleasure and fun, the benefits to the child can be enormous in terms of motivation, self-esteem, developing relationships, developing communication and teamwork skills and taking responsibility. Often there is a knock-on positive effect which carries over into school and other aspects of the child's life. But if the foster carer doesn't suggest joining a club or doing an out-of-school activity, it may not occur to a child in care to ask or even to want to do this. They may lack confidence. They may have no idea of what they could do. Or they may assume there is no money to pay for it, or that getting permission to do it would involve too much hassle, or that it would be too difficult to get there. It's important for "corporate parents" to find out what the child might enjoy and to make it happen.

> *As a group, children in care underachieve. As individuals, like all young people, they have hidden talents. Some will only discover what they are good at or passionate about out of school. Unless we know what motivates each young person, how are we going to help them reach their potential?*
>
> *(ContinYou, 2005)*

TIP 2

Assess the impact of the child's history on her education

Make a flow chart of the child's life

Drawing up a flow chart of events in the child's life can be an illuminating exercise for a social worker. For example, there may be an assumption that because the child was with her mother for the first two or three years of her life, this was a period of stability for her. But in fact, by looking at everything that happened to the child (or at least everything you can find out), you might discover that, for instance, she had to move with her mother to a refuge because of domestic violence, followed by a return to the family home, then perhaps a spell living with her mother and grandmother while her mother was suffering from mental health problems. So in fact, her life may have been anything but stable.

Where there are gaps in what is known or can be found out about the child's life, leave the gaps in the chart – and assume that "Here be dragons".

Analyse everything you know about the child's history in terms of its impact on her education

If you find out, for example, that a child was born eight weeks prematurely and didn't leave hospital until she was 12 months old, this could go a long way to explaining her educational difficulties.

Early home environment

If it has been necessary to remove a child from her family, almost by definition her early home environment is unlikely to have been conducive to her intellectual development. The child's "communication environment" – which means how much parents talk to and read to their children at home – really matters.

> *We have found overwhelming evidence that children's life chances are most heavily predicated on their development in the first five years of life.*
>
> *(Field, 2010, quoted in Centre Forum, 2011)*

In its report on the impact of the home learning environment on children's learning and social mobility, Centre Forum quoted a striking study carried out in the US that looked at the number of words children heard in the family home, comparing welfare-dependent family homes with working-class families and professional families:

> *This study identified that a child in a welfare-dependent family home hears on average 616 words*

> *an hour; for a child in a working-class home, the figure is around double (1,251 words); and for a child in a professional home, it is 2,153 words an hour. Furthermore, in a typical hour, the child in the welfare-dependent family home will hear on average five positive affirmations and 11 negative prohibitions; the child from the working-class home 12 affirmations and seven prohibitions; and the child in the professional home will hear 32 positive affirmations to only five negative prohibitions.*
>
> *(Centre Forum, 2011)*

When the figures were extrapolated to the first four years of life, children in the "professional" families had heard 45 million words, while children in "welfare" families had heard just 13 million.

Children who have spent their pre-school years in a less than ideal home environment, from which they are later removed, are likely to have been disadvantaged in terms of their language development and communication skills. Poor language development in toddlers is likely to mean they are behind their peers when they start school. The long-term effects can be far-reaching.

> *A recent Department for Education report has identified that children's language development at the age of two is very strongly associated with performance across all subject areas upon entering primary school...*
>
> *(Roulstone et al, 2011, quoted in Centre Forum, 2011)*

Unaccompanied asylum-seeking children and young people

There will inevitably be much that is not known about the child's early life if she (or, more often, he) came to the UK unaccompanied to seek asylum. Some children and young people may not have been able to attend school for long in their home countries, if at all, and are likely to have had long periods out of school. However, some will have had several years of education and come from families which have placed a high value on education and qualifications. Some families will have risked a great deal to send their child to safety in the UK and urged them to work hard for the chance of a better life.

Many children and young people in this situation will be highly motivated to work hard and to achieve at school when they come to the UK. However, many of these children and young people will be traumatised by their experiences in their home country, and their long and hazardous journey to the UK, and face the challenge of adjusting to a completely strange environment, far from home and family, and the shock of a new and alien culture. They may speak little or no English. Even if they did well at school in their country of origin, their school experience in the UK is likely to be very different in many ways. For some, even if they are highly motivated to learn, there will still be some barriers in their way – social workers, foster carers and teachers will need to work hard on their behalf if they are to overcome these obstacles.

Missing school means missing out

Some children will have had frequent or long absences from school before being taken into care, and this will clearly affect their chances of keeping up with their peers.

However, social workers need to do everything they can to make sure the child does not continue to miss out on her schooling *after* being taken into care. You will, of course, avoid moving a child from a school where she is doing well. But if you have no choice but to move the child to a placement that will require a change of school, you need to ensure that you have sorted out a school place in advance. Having a school place ready and waiting should be a priority when making

23

plans for her to move anywhere.

Long absences can cause a child to fall behind and, without extra help, it can then be very difficult to catch up.

Some social workers say: 'We'll just put a few hours a week of home tuition in place until a school place becomes available'. But this will never meet a child's needs. Children need to be in school, with everything that goes with it, to get the full benefit from the education they are entitled to. Every day that they are out of school means that they will find it that much harder to fit in and keep up when they are back in school. Being at home rather than in school also puts great pressure on the relationship with the foster carers, and could put the foster placement at risk.

The Who Cares? Trust questions whether all looked after children are able to access the education they are entitled to.

> *All children should be able to go to school for 190 days a year. Research has shown in the past that looked after children miss out on some of the schooling they are entitled to due to placement moves, exclusions from school and the provision of unsuitable alternative education. We want to investigate whether there is a group of looked after children for whom the state is failing to provide a meaningful, full-time education.*
>
> *(Online poll, www.thewhocarestrust.org.uk, accessed 29.10.12)*

If the child has to start at a new school, make every effort to ensure she can start at the "right" time. Starting in the middle of the school year marks her out as different and can make it harder for her both in terms of school work and, of course, establishing friendships. Friendship groups will have already formed and in some cases, joining the class late could make the child more vulnerable to bullying. These difficulties could lead to other issues such as the child refusing to go to school or developing school phobia.

In care, in school: what's it like for a child?

Here are just a few things about being "in care" that can make school life difficult for a looked after child or young person.

- The stigma of being "in care", which can extend to bullying. In some cases, even teachers might have prejudices around the fact that the child is "in care", or that her birth relatives are known locally for being a "problem family" or for their criminal activity. These prejudices could colour the teacher's expectations of what the child might be capable of achieving at school.

- The child may be unsure of how or how much to tell her schoolmates about her past, or the fact that she is in care. She may share too much, and then find they fail to respect confidences or use the information to bully her.

- Children removed from home because of abuse may continue to fear their abuser, e.g. that he might meet them at the school gate or on the way home.

- Lessons on certain subjects can be upsetting for a child or young person in care, for example, being asked to bring in a photograph of themselves as a baby (she may not have any); to write an autobiography; to write an essay entitled "My family" or "What I did in the holidays"; or to design a family tree.

- Lessons on genetics, sex education and drugs education may remind a child or young person (e.g. one who has been sexually abused or whose parents misuse drugs) of behaviour of people in their family or other abusers. A child who has suffered sexual abuse may be much more knowledgeable than her peers and make inappropriate comments in lessons, or may be upset by the lesson's content.

- Some children's books deal with the subject of being in care, and in some texts the child character may be threatened with "going into care" as a punishment.

To help teachers and others to understand what is going on and how best to help the child manage the things she finds difficult, see Tip 6 on forming and maintaining a relationship with the key people in the school.

Be aware of any impending transitions for the child

Times of transition mean that a child who finds it hard to regulate stress is put under even more stress – see Tip 9 for suggestions about supporting a child through transitions.

There are some obvious transitions such as moving between schools, moving from primary to secondary school, or from lower school to upper school. But in planning or review meetings when you are considering impending transitions, everyone needs to be aware of the significance of other events for the child. A new school year, for example, can mean an unfamiliar teacher, a different classroom and sometimes new classmates. A favourite teacher or teaching assistant or a close school friend may be leaving the school – a significant loss for a child or young person.

Don't forget that the summer holidays in themselves represent a big transition for a child. The child and foster carers are moving from a situation in which instead of spending a few hours a day together, they are spending all day, every day, for six weeks. This can place additional pressures on the relationship. Trying to keep the child constructively occupied and entertained for such a long period can be challenging for a foster carer.

Another type of transition is that which is caused by turbulence in the network around the child.

Turbulence in the child's network

Some local councils, tasked with reducing their spending, have made cuts to their provision for children and families. A report from the Family and Parenting Institute looked at spending in eight local authorities in 2011/12 and 2012/13 and its findings point to a squeeze on funding for universal services. It found that the sharpest reduction in spending has been in services that councils provide to schools (such as school improvement and education welfare).

Spending on those "non-social work" services most associated with universal provision to families and

> *young people (such as youth centres and early years provision in children's centres) also shouldered a large share of spending reductions. Councils were increasingly refocusing limited resources on targeted intervention.*
>
> *(Family and Parenting Institute, 2012)*

What this means is that many of the activities, events and play schemes that would have previously made life more enjoyable for the child and easier for the carer are no more. When the cuts fall on services like this, children's sense of a strong local support network may be threatened. They miss out on opportunities for new experiences, fun, physical activity, friendships and beneficial relationships with adult leaders. In some areas there is little or no provision for children during the summer holidays – and this often impacts most severely on the most vulnerable.

Foster carers themselves are likely to feel less supported when services and provision are withdrawn and therefore less able to cope well. And of course the children they care for may well be able to sense this.

Where clubs and associations do survive, e.g. the Brownies, Scouts, Sea Cadets, children's football clubs, etc, they can be important for holding things together in a local community.

Turbulence in schools

Bear in mind that the child's school itself may be going through a turbulent period. Many schools are turning into academies, a process that can produce uncertainty and anxiety among teaching and support staff. Some teachers have found their conditions of service have worsened and new demands are made by school managers, including performance management measures which affect morale and can even impact on their pay-scale. Structural changes in a school or local authority, changes in support services, redundancies and burnout among teaching and support staff can all have both a direct and indirect impact on the pupils.

Also, be aware of the possibility of secondary traumatic stress in adults in the child's network – see Tip 6. This is related to living or working closely with a traumatised child or young person. (It is different from burnout, which is employment related or role related and is linked to negative factors in the work environment such as lack of or loss of support.)

Repeat this exercise at every review of the care plan

As you can see, important aspects of the child's school life can change significantly in the space of a few months even without a major change such as moving school, so it would be a good idea to consider and make a note of any impending transition at every review of the care plan. It need not take long – and the process of updating it will alert you to any issues that you, the foster carers and the child's teachers need to be aware of.

TIP 3

Gather information about the child's education history

Gathering information about the child's education history, and also maintaining this information and keeping it up to date, is very important.

Initially, you may need to contact the child's previous schools (or ask the current school to do this) in order to access his education records – be ready to explain why it is important, and to persevere in your attempts to gather this information.

Looking at his records will tell you about when the child's problems (if any) originated, which other agencies have been involved with him (e.g. Child and Adolescent Mental Health Services (CAMHS)) and about any earlier interventions in terms of behavioural support, for example. Some children have a thick file which spells out everything schools have tried in attempts to modify their behaviour.

> *Mandy joined the school in Year 9. It took three months to persuade her previous schools to hand over their records. But when they did, it made for interesting reading: previous schools had started the "statementing" procedures five times, but each time Mandy's mother had whisked her away from the school. Mandy's mum never told the new school about what had gone before. Each new school was to be a "fresh start" and no information had been passed on.*

You need to gather information about:

● the child's experience of pre-school education, if any;

● schools the child has attended, and dates;

● the outcome of the child's education to date – SATs results and any other test or exam results;

● the child's identified special educational needs, if any;

● anyone important to the child in relation to their education.

For example, you might find that his SATs results were poor, and teachers may be assuming he is not very bright – but if you also discover that he had spent the previous three months out of school, this helps to put his poor results in context and shows that they are less about his ability and more about the time that he has missed.

Some of this information can form part of the child's Personal Education Plan (PEP).

The Personal Education Plan

Everyone hates paperwork, but the Personal Education Plan (PEP) should not be just a paper exercise. The PEP provides a forum for social workers and education professionals to meet, together with the child, in the interests of that child.

When a child becomes looked after, it is up to you as the child's social worker to inform the child's school. Every child taken into the care system must have a PEP and this must be completed within 20 days of going into care. (This means the PEP should be ready in time for the first review.)

As the social worker, you should trigger or initiate the PEP, and to complete it you work in partnership with:

● the child or young person;

● the designated teacher at the school (see below);

● the child's carer;

● the child's parent or relevant family member;

● any other relevant agency involved, perhaps including someone from the virtual school team (see below).

The PEP:

● contains some of the child's social care information (the child's legal status and whatever part of the history is appropriate to share with the school);

● sets out clear targets and actions (the designated teacher or someone representing him or her should lead on identifying and setting attainment targets);

● records the child's achievements, results and attendance;

● records information about special educational needs if the child is on the special needs register (see below);

● records information about the child's out-of-school activities, interests and achievements;

● is an opportunity for the child to state and write down their views, hopes and worries about school, what they would like to do in terms of out-of-school learning and activities, and their aspirations for the future;

● may record how the Pupil Premium (see Tip 6) is spent.

The child should be involved in a sensitive, meaningful and constructive way.

You may want to add to the PEP information on strategies that work with this particular child, for example, that he sometimes needs a quiet place to retreat to when he is getting stressed or angry, so that he can calm down.

The PEP should be reviewed at least biannually. However, one of the recommendations in a report by an independent cross-party inquiry into the educational attainment of looked after children in England is that:

> *Personal Education Plans (PEPs) should be reviewed termly rather than biannually and should not be restricted to the period of compulsory education but should transcend a child's time in care. The 0–25 model adopted by Hackney should be the norm.*
>
> *(All-Party Parliamentary Group for Looked After Children and Care Leavers, 2012)*

Bear in mind that some children and young people will not welcome the idea of attending a meeting in school with their social worker as this marks them out as different from their peers and attracts negative attention. If the child or young person you are working with feels like this, explore whether it might be possible to have the meeting at a time when the child's friends won't miss him or notice he has gone, e.g. after school.

Designated teacher

All schools have to appoint a "designated teacher" to promote the educational achievement of looked after children on the school roll. The designated teacher helps write the PEP, advises others in the school on appropriate strategies to assist learning and liaises with others outside the school in respect of looked after children.

Virtual schools

A "virtual school" is a team, led by a virtual school headteacher, which is part of the local authority. It champions the education of the authority's looked after children wherever they are, whether within the authority or outside it, in schools or in residential care. Virtual school staff are usually qualified teachers and can provide advice, guidance, training and professional development for anyone concerned with the educational needs of looked after children. They liaise and work with designated teachers in schools in and out of the area. They work in different ways, but most will be able to advise on a range of issues including special needs provision, behaviour management, admissions, exclusion, alternative education provision, PEPs, attendance, progress, transitions, funding and achievement. Some provide one-to-one support for children who are struggling or who have fallen behind with their lessons. Remember that you can contact the virtual school head teacher if you have any questions or concerns about finding a school place, or if the child is at risk of exclusion, or any other aspect of a looked after child's education.

Virtual school heads are a key way in which a local authority can demonstrate that it is meeting its legal duty to promote the educational achievement of the children it looks after. However, some local authorities are cutting back on their virtual school teams because of pressure on their budgets.

Special educational need/inclusion

The term "special educational need" covers a wide range of conditions such as learning difficulties, attention deficit hyperactivity disorder (ADHD), dyslexia, autism, speech and language difficulties, as well as severe behaviour problems, and so on. The term "inclusion" refers to the process of helping children with these difficulties to thrive in a mainstream school.

Some children with severe learning difficulties, severe physical disabilities or severe emotional and behavioural difficulties need to attend special schools that can cater for their needs. Others with less severe problems can attend mainstream schools, with extra support.

Many mainstream schools have units attached to them to allow them to provide extra support and individual programmes of work for certain children, e.g. units for children who have language difficulties or are hearing impaired, and pupil referral units for children who have been truanting or whose behaviour cannot be managed in the classroom.

Every school has to have a special needs department – sometimes called an inclusion department – with a special educational needs co-ordinator (SENCO) or a teacher in charge of inclusion. A percentage of the devolved school grant (the money the Government provides for the running of the school) is used to address special educational needs.

Statements: the system is changing

At the time of writing (December 2012), the local authority has to issue a statement of special educational needs if requested by the child's parents or headteacher (or, if it declines that request, parents can appeal via the SEN tribunal system). Being "statemented" can be a lengthy business but it is the trigger for extra support, usually covering every aspect of the child's education including NHS therapies, speech and language therapy, and so on.

Within the provision for special educational needs, children currently receive different levels of support depending on the severity of their problems. If you are the social worker for a child with a statement of special educational needs, you will want to know what level of support the child is on.

However, the system is set to change. The Government wants to replace statements with "single plans" covering education, health and social care, which will extend from birth to age 25 as long as a young person remains in education or training.

A Special Educational Needs Green Paper was laid down in September 2012, for implementation in 2014. Entitled *Support and Aspiration:*

A new approach to special educational needs (Department for Education, 2012b), it sets out a plan for a multi-agency assessment of need to replace the previous system of statementing. Under the proposed new system, from 2014 there will be a plan which covers education, health and social care for every child with special educational need. There will be a single assessment process.

(At the time of writing, the Government's draft legislation is being considered by the Education Select Committee.)

IPSEA (Independent Parental Special Education Advice, see *Useful Organisations*) issued this statement in October 2012 in response to the proposed changes:

> *As currently drafted, these provisions do not fully retain the current legal entitlement of children with special educational needs to have their needs assessed and then met.*
>
> *Most notably, parents acting for their children lose the specific right to request assessment for their child and for that request to be responded to by their local authority, the first stage in obtaining a statement of special educational needs, renamed a Plan in the draft Bill.*
>
> *Secondly, the draft provisions change the wording for the way these Plans must be written. This potentially weakens the requirement to describe the support the child needs in detail such that everyone concerned can understand who should do what, when, how long for and how often. Without this "specification", no one can ensure the child gets the help they need.*
>
> *These two issues, together with the loss of many protective details in current legislation, mean that*

> *the draft provisions currently do not live up to the commitment that ministers have made to ensure statutory rights are protected.*
>
> *IPSEA does welcome the extension of the age range to be covered by the replacement to statements, the application of direct legal duties to academies (including free schools), and the power to pilot the child's right of appeal outlined in the draft provisions.*
>
> *However, this remains essentially a system focused on education support. Health and social services are not given any new direct duties to meet children's needs, and assessment of needs stays fragmented and lacks independence. In addition, disabled children/young people without SEN are not covered at all.*
>
> *(IPSEA, 2012)*

Social workers advocating for a child with special educational needs will need to get to grips with the new system, when it is finalised and implemented, and work out its implications for the child.

Writing in *The Guardian*, John Harris, the father of an autistic son, said he fears the proposed changes:

> *Under the current system, local authorities have a duty to specify the provision that will be made...the new plans contain only an obligation to "set out" what will be provided...*
>
> *In the switch from statements of educational needs to the new single plans, there is another glaring*

problem. Under the current system, all of a child's therapies and programmes – even if they're provided by the NHS – come under the umbrella heading of "education" and thereby fall under the remit of the SEN tribunal. If something fails to materialise or is taken away, you can at least take your case to an affordable(ish) forum of appeal. But no more: the Government plans to separate everything out into three categories of education, health and social care – but keep only the first one under the tribunal's authority. What that means for parents like me is obvious enough: the knocking-away of accountability that currently underlies things such as occupational therapy and help with our children's speech and language.

(Harris, 2012)

The Department for Education's response to concerns expressed by John Harris concluded: 'These reforms will put parents in charge, giving them better information and a comprehensive package of support that meets their needs.'

Find out about anyone important to the child in relation to their education

Some relationships can be extremely supportive to the child's educational progress – for instance, a child's grandmother may regularly read him bedtime stories, or a teenager's best friend may meet up with her every night to do homework together.

When a looked after child finds it hard to cope with the stress of school, it can be helpful if there is a particular adult within the school whom the child trusts to be a "safe person" in a "safe place". This may be the class teacher, a teacher with responsibility for pastoral care or a school counsellor, but it could well be someone else that the child has "chosen" for himself. A teaching assistant can play an important role in providing stability for a child who finds it hard to organise himself, for instance, meeting him off the school bus and making sure he has all the right books and equipment for the day's lessons.

If there is such an attachment figure in the school and they are available and committed to the role, this would be a compelling reason to keep the child in a particular school rather than moving him.

TIP 4

Get to know the carers and work with them

In 2012, the Office of the Children's Rights Director for England took a group of looked after children to talk to the then Children's Minister, Tim Loughton, about their education. What the children said made it clear:

> *...that the help a child in care gets with their education depends very much on where they are placed and the carers they are placed with...that their carers have responsibility for them, and they make a huge difference to children's education.*

One child said:

> *My carer is lovely, tries to discuss things with me and talks about my education and which route I am going to take. It helps when they are around to speak to.*
>
> *(Office of the Children's Rights Director for England, 2012)*

The impact of carers on the child's education starts very early on – even pre-school, if the child goes into care at a young age. Thinking about the importance of the pre-school home environment for the child's intellectual development (see Tip 2), find out whether the carers talk and listen to her a lot. Do they understand the importance for pre-school children of learning through play? Do they read to her, sing songs together and recite nursery rhymes to her? Do they do stimulating activities with her, inside and outside the home? Do they make learning fun? Are there plenty of books and educational toys in the home?

With older children, do the foster carers take an interest in what the child is learning at school, discuss her homework with her and help her to develop motivation, a work ethic and good study skills? Are they patient and supportive if she is struggling to learn something? Do they show that they support the school, and ensure that she is out of school as little as possible?

What is the carer's educational history and attitude to education?

When it comes to education, foster carers have a vital part to play as role models for children and young people of all ages, supporting them and encouraging their motivation. Getting to know the child's carers will help you to understand their relationship with the child and to value the unique gifts they bring to their role. It will also help you to recognise any warning signs that they are beginning to suffer from stress or secondary trauma.

Recognise that even if the carer has had adverse experiences of education and has only bad memories of school life, he or she can put this to positive use to support a looked after child. If a carer has worked through their experiences and is able to truthfully say, for example, 'I wish I'd worked harder at school and not messed around so much', they can be an effective champion for the child.

However, not all carers are interested in supporting the child's education – they may see it as a low priority, compared with other issues for the child. They may have fairly low aspirations for him or her in terms of academic achievement.

Dan's carers, like many who provide temporary homes for the rapidly rising number of children in care, didn't flourish themselves academically. They view schools as all the same and books as boring. They don't press him to do his homework as 'The poor lad's got enough on his plate already'. Besides, they don't think he's going to be with them for long, as they're finding his behaviour challenging.

What Dan needs is a stable placement with carers who believe in education.

(Northen, 2011)

If you feel that the child's foster carers have an unhelpful attitude towards education, you need to discuss this with the fostering service provider. Fostering service providers are responsible for ensuring that carers promote the child's education as well as her physical and emotional well-being.

Sometimes a foster carer's underlying ambivalence towards school only becomes apparent at times of stress when the child is having problems at school.

The value of foster carers who are still learning

Do the carers read for pleasure? Are they studying? Do they use the library? Their own learning, interests and hobbies are an important part of what they can offer the child. Their own children can also be helpful here.

Most foster carers go on courses to develop their own skills – and, for the child, seeing their carer or the carer's children studying, reading and writing essays, or using the computer for research, sends a positive message. Some children who struggle to concentrate on homework will find it much easier if they can work alongside someone else at the kitchen table, for instance.

Carers who are themselves continuing to learn are excellent role models, and it hardly matters what they are learning, whether it's cake decorating, football refereeing, playing the guitar, dance classes or computer literacy. Any interest the carer shows in studying, taking classes or developing their own skills demonstrates to the child the pleasure of learning and improving. Value what the carers have to offer – and if necessary, help them to realise its value too.

Encourage the carers to use the facilities and resources available to them

Discuss with the carers how they could encourage the child's learning and extracurricular activities. Encourage them to make use of everything that is on offer for the child. For example, is there a toy library they could use? What about the local library? Some libraries have story-time sessions for younger children. Some local authorities offer vouchers that allow looked after children to enjoy local leisure facilities such as swimming pools, sports centres, museums and art galleries for free or at a discounted rate. Is there a homework club at the school or the local library? What activities and clubs are there locally, e.g. art clubs, Brownies, Guides and Scouts, Duke of Edinburgh's Award Scheme, choirs, children's theatre, volunteering in the local community? Which ones might appeal to him most, and what financial and practical support would be needed for him to take part? A shy child might be more likely to try a new club if he can go along with a friend.

What do carers need in order to support the child to take part in out-of-school activities?

Some carers will be aware of the range of activities available in the local community, but others won't be. They need up-to-date information on "what's on" – both school-based and community provision.

- *Foster carers may have children of their own who are pursuing different activities – can their children be included in the same activities?*

- *Some carers may not value a wide enough range of activities, or have had experience of them, so may need encouragement and persuasion.*

- *Carers may perceive leisure activities as posing an additional burden on them and, therefore, they may need general support in understanding and supporting children's behavioural and emotional needs.*

(ContinYou, 2005)

THE LETTERBOX CLUB

Around 120 local authorities now subscribe to the Letterbox Club, an educational support programme in which over 5,000 looked after children are enrolled. Children aged seven to 13 receive free books and other educational materials in a parcel in the post, to encourage them to enjoy reading stories and playing number games with their carers. Some participating local authorities add into the parcel details of the child's local library and any summer schemes, half-term events, homework clubs and so on.

The Letterbox Club is managed by Booktrust, in partnership with the University of Leicester. For more information, see www.letterboxclub.org.uk.

Fostering Education course

A course for foster carers has achieved some success in improving the reading skills of looked after children. The Fostering Education project was piloted by BAAF in 2010 with 60 sets of foster carers and children, and taught carers a technique called "paired reading". Researchers found that the children's reading accuracy and comprehension improved at almost twice the rate of other reading schemes.

> *Southwark foster carer Greta Bent, 53, says the techniques she learned on the Fostering Education course have radically improved the reading ability of the seven-year-old boy she looks after. Before the course, he had the reading ability of a five-year-old. Now, she says, he's devouring Harry Potter books and his reading age is about eight or nine years old. Greta is a fan of paired reading, which she found easy to learn.*
>
> *His frustration diminished as his reading got better and as a result his behaviour improved too. Greta says the parts of the course on dealing with children's anger were invaluable.*
>
> *(Stothart, 2011)*

The Fostering Education course manual, entitled *Supporting Children's Learning* (Pallett *et al*, 2010) was distributed free to all local authorities to enable them to run the 10-week course for their own foster carers. All that local authorities need to supply is a venue, two trainers and the photocopying. Why not ask whether your local authority will run this course for foster carers?

Ensure carers understand their responsibilities in relation to the child's schoolwork

Foster carers should provide all the help and encouragement that a caring parent would provide, such as the suggestions below.

● Ensure that the child attends school regularly and gets to school on time and is ready to learn.

● Listen to her read, support her with homework, check that she has done and handed in her homework, and sign the homework diary if there is one.

● Help her organise herself so that she takes the right books, sports kit and anything else she needs to school each day.

● Ensure the child has the equipment and resources she needs and a suitable space in a quiet room to study and do homework.

● Attend school events and parents' evenings (unless it has been agreed that someone else, e.g. the child's parent or social worker, will attend instead).

● Communicate with the teachers about any learning, emotional, social or behavioural problems she is having.

● Show the child that they expect her to work hard and to do well.

● Celebrate her successes both in and out of school, whether it's earning a sticker from the teacher for "trying hard", doing well in a test, performing in the school play, playing for the school netball team – or simply staying out of trouble for a whole week.

The duties of the fostering service provider

1. *The fostering service provider must promote the educational achievement of children placed with foster parents.*

2. In particular, the fostering service provider must:

- *implement a procedure for monitoring the educational achievement, progress and school attendance of children placed with foster parents;*

- *promote the regular school attendance and participation in school activities of children of compulsory school age placed with foster parents, and;*

- *provide foster parents with such information and assistance, including equipment, as may be necessary to meet the educational needs of children placed with them.*

3. The fostering service provider must ensure that any education they provide for any child placed with a foster parent who is of compulsory school age, but who is not attending school, is efficient and suitable to the child's age, ability, aptitude, and any special educational needs the child may have.

4. The fostering service provider must ensure that foster parents promote the leisure interests of children placed with them.

5. Where any child placed with a foster parent is above compulsory school age, the fostering service provider must assist with the making of, and give effect to, the arrangements made for the child's education, training and employment.

(From the Fostering Services (England) Regulations 2011)

Who does what?

The precise sharing out of responsibilities of social workers, foster carers and others (such as designated teachers) in supporting the education of looked after children will vary. Some are clear, e.g. the foster carer's role in making sure the child has a quiet place to do homework and so on. Others are more complicated and depend on factors such as the child's status (e.g. when the child first comes into care; when there is a care order; when the child is returning home), and the different local commissioning arrangements that apply with the particular fostering provider.

It might be a useful exercise for you, as the child's social worker, to go through the following checklist of tasks and consider "who does what" and give it to the foster carer so that she can be clear about what is expected of her. (Many of these responsibilities are shared or negotiated, and you can indicate that on the checklist too.) You could complete the checklist at the placement planning meeting or at any other time.

Task	Social worker	Foster carer	Designated teacher
Who...			
Initially chooses a school/early years place?			
Chooses a school at normal transfer times?			
Appeals for a place?			
Asks the local authority to provide education while a child waits for a place (if necessary)?			
Buys the uniform?			

Pays for school transport?			
Signs the home–school agreement?			
Ensures good time-keeping and attendance?			
Contacts the school if the child is off sick?			
Checks homework diaries?			
Provides a quiet place for homework?			
Helps the child with homework?			
Attends parents' evening?			
Arranges work experience?			
Agrees support and targets on the PEP?			
Clarifies arrangements for signing permission slips?			
Signs permission slips?			
Pays for school trips?			
Buys computer equipment?			

Ensures computer equipment, etc, has parental controls?			
Complains about bullying?			
Asks for help for a child with special educational needs?			
Appeals if help is not forthcoming?			
Attends their annual review?			
Contributes to a pastoral support programme?			
Makes representations about an exclusion?			
Asks the school to provide homework for an excluded child?			
Asks the local authority to provide education for a permanently excluded child?			
Advises the child when making subject choices?			
Supports the child when applying for further/higher education?			

Support carers when decisions by schools and education officials need to be challenged

Sometimes, of course, social workers will need to advocate for the child and support foster carers, for example, in challenging an exclusion or trying to obtain an assessment for the child. This can result in social workers challenging the local authority which is their own employer.

Beth (not her real name) is a foster carer in the south-west of England. In her experience, if the local authority needs to be challenged over decisions about looked after children's education, some social workers may be reluctant to do this:

'I had a child who was out of school. Everything he needed was written into his statement. We were advised of the school the education department was proposing to send him to and I said: "They won't be able to meet his needs". For example, it said he should have a designated space to cool off and the school didn't have such a space. The child started at the school and it was a disaster. Then I found that the LEA had taken out of the statement all the things that the school couldn't provide. Social workers were reluctant to do anything so I found a solicitor. He said this was a common problem – social workers would be getting into a battle with their employer and they think it will cause them difficulty.

'Quite often foster children don't get excluded but instead they get sent home to "cool off" so it doesn't register as an actual exclusion. Schools shouldn't be doing this. I have found social workers reluctant to speak out about things like this. I also think a lot of social workers get very little training and input on education law so they don't say to the school: "We shouldn't be having another exclusion now". But I can see their difficulty if they make big waves.

'Perhaps there should be more external support for foster carers. I live in one local authority and foster for a neighbouring local authority. In the local authority that I foster for, all the fostering staff are in the same office and sit alongside the education staff, so I didn't feel it was independent. But in the local authority I live in, there is an educational support organisation funded by several local authorities and they were able to offer me support. And of course, if you are fostering for an independent agency the situation is not so difficult. I have also found IPSEA –

Independent Parental Special Education Advice – absolutely fantastic and they can provide all the information about how many exclusions are allowed, test cases about school transport and so on. They offer some fantastic training too.'

(IPSEA is a national charity providing free legally based advice to families who have children with special educational needs. See *Useful Organisations*.)

What are the carers' attitudes to the internet, e-safety and social networking websites?

Using the internet is an important part of school and homework even in primary schools, so children need access to the internet. Many older children see social networking websites like Facebook as vital for their friendships and social life. Looked after children and young people need to have the same opportunities as their peers to enjoy all that the online world has to offer and to develop the digital skills that everyone now needs. But who is making sure the child is safe while using the internet and social networking sites? Many looked after children and young people have particular vulnerabilities that could put them at even more risk than their peers when using the internet.

E-safety is an important aspect of keeping children and young people of all ages safe from harm. As the child's or young person's social worker, you need to find out how much she knows about issues such as e-safety, how to protect her personal information online and how to avoid falling prey to scams, cyberbullies, harmful websites, sexual exploitation and grooming on the internet. What devices does she have access to which allow her to go on the internet? Laptops, some televisions, smartphones, ipads, ipods and games consoles can be used to connect to the internet – do the carers understand this? Do these devices all have parental controls set up on them? How is the child using the internet – is she playing online games, and if so, who with? Does she access the internet outside the foster home, for instance, at school, at friends' houses, in the library or at an internet café on the way home from school? Does she use social networking sites? What is her attitude to risk and personal safety online?

The child's school may well have provided lessons and guidance on this, but a looked after child may have missed out on that part of the curriculum because of absence or simply not taking in the information. Few children and young people are likely to have had advice or guidance from a parent on this subject before becoming looked after, so carers have a vital role in helping to educate children in their care about the safe use of the internet and social networking websites. But foster carers have widely varying levels of knowledge in this area. While some will be avid users themselves and will be able to talk to the child or young person about e-safety, behaviour on social networking sites, etc, others lack confidence and knowledge. The risk then is that they either fail to address the issue or decide it's "safer" not to let the child use the internet at all. Children in care shouldn't simply be given free rein to explore the internet, with no guidance, supervision or control being applied to their activities online. But nor should they be banned by anxious foster carers from using the internet at home – that is likely to simply drive them to use it in secret, outside the home, with no opportunity for dialogue between the carers and the child.

Cyberbullying

Cyberbullying – bullying, threats or harassment by peers via text messaging, emails or social networking sites – can be an isolating and frightening experience and, in severe cases, can wreck young people's lives. Tragically, there have been some cases in which young people have committed suicide as a result of being bullied in this way. Foster carers need to know how to help young people deal with cyberbullying, for example, reassuring them; reporting it to the school and the relevant mobile phone provider or social networking site; advising them not to reply to messages but to save them in case they are later needed as evidence for an investigation by the school or even the police; "blocking" the offender and possibly changing the phone number; and so on.

An important part of carers' ability to help a young person in distress for any reason is, of course, to develop a relationship of trust in the hope that she will feel able to turn to them for help when anxious, scared or out of her depth.

Local authorities providing laptop computers to looked after children and young people should ensure that these are set up with "safe search" and parental control software which is appropriate to the child's age and stage. However, some young people complain that the filters and security software installed on laptops provided by the local authority circumscribe their internet access so much that they don't bother using the laptop any more.

It's true that many children and young people are more knowledgeable than their carers when it comes to technical skills (and some will find ways of circumventing any parental controls). However, many looked after children and young people lack the maturity and the social and emotional intelligence to safely navigate the risks of the online world, so it is vital that a responsible adult takes an interest and talks to them about these issues. Ideally, this will be the foster carer, supplementing information the child is given in school.

Many foster carers will need training and support in order to do this properly. Some social workers, too, feel that they need support to get up to speed on understanding e-safety and the implications of social networking. Some local authorities and other organisations are developing their guidelines and policies in this rapidly changing area. Some provide in-house training for their social workers and foster carers, while others are putting on training days and workshops (e.g. led by trainers from organisations such as BAAF or CEOP, or Eileen Fursland, author of this book and BAAF's guide for foster carers, *Foster Care and Social Networking* (Fursland, 2011)). Policies, guidelines and training for foster carers should cover issues such as:

- internet safety for children and young people and effective approaches to reducing the risks for the child or young person in care. The expectations placed on carers in terms of supervision should acknowledge what is realistic and appropriate in a family home;

- "safe caring" issues and precautions around the use of computers in the foster placement, including the carer's and carer's children's own use of social networking;

- finding a balance between protecting the child and allowing her the opportunity to learn about the internet, develop her skills and become "internet-savvy";

- implications of behaviour on social networking sites, the risks of giving out personal information, online privacy, "oversharing" and confidentiality, as well as issues such as "sexting" and cyberbullying;

- contact with birth family members via social networking sites – in particular, the vital issue of unmediated contact for those children and young people for whom contact is meant to be supervised or is not supposed to take place at all.

For more information on e-safety, see Fursland, 2011, and *Useful Resources*.

TIP 5

Find out as much as possible about the school

Generally speaking, stability is beneficial for children. Too many looked after children's lives are disrupted by changes of school and the resultant damage to learning, friendships and relationships. Most social workers would quite rightly try to avoid moving a child from one school to another (and would resist pressure from a school to move the child) unless there was a very good reason, for example, if the child needed to be placed in a different area for his own safety.

However, it's important not to be tied to diktats – in a small number of cases, a fresh start in a new school can be what an individual child needs at a particular time.

You may be planning for a change of school for a particular child (because he needs to move to a new area, is at a transitional stage, e.g. primary to secondary, or for some other reason). Or alternatively, you may be supporting a child who has just come into care but is staying in the same school with no imminent moves.

If a child has just come into care and will be staying in the same school, you will need to form and maintain a relationship with key people who are involved with him at school (see Tip 6). You will also want to find out how the child is doing at school, whether he is happy there and what problems he has, if any. You'll want to be sure the school knows as much as they need to know about the child's circumstances and difficulties, and find out what support they are able to offer.

What is your role?

If the child's parents have retained parental responsibility, you may have to consult them about the choice of school and other matters. You will also need to consult the child's carers, who are likely to have a preference about the choice of school (see below). And, of course, don't forget the child himself – he may have strong views, particularly when it comes to which secondary school he attends. However, you should remember that the child needs you to be a strong advocate for him just as a good, caring parent would be.

A large element of the "school choice" model involves parents actively evaluating different school options, selecting the best option, and then advocating on behalf of their child throughout their school career. Parents play a central role in holding the school to account, in appealing against exclusions, and in making sure children get to school in the first place.

Yet it is often unclear exactly who the "parent" for looked after children is. Children may have contact with a wide range of professionals, in addition to a foster carer. And individual roles can become confused, with the risk that key duties fall between agencies and are unfulfilled. During the transition from primary to secondary school, for example, social workers can be unclear about their responsibilities. Children who have experienced multiple placements or have changed placement prior to starting school may also suffer from a lack of adequate planning and preparation, and there is a danger that they are placed with the closest school, or the easiest to access, rather than the one which best meets their needs.

(Chater and Le Grand, 2006)

Is this the right school for the child?

In some small towns and villages, there may be only one school and no other options. However, if you live in a town or city where there are two or more local schools, try to form a good general idea of what the different ones are like. Then, when you are considering which would be the right school for a particular child, you can do more detailed research and consider each school from the point of view of how well it would suit that individual child.

It's never as simple as sending the child to the closest school, unless there is genuinely no other choice in that specific location. Choice of school is a decision that could have far-reaching consequences for the child, so you owe it to him to consider it carefully.

Check out all available sources of information on the school

Finding out information about different schools can take some time and effort, and could be difficult to fit into a busy social work schedule. Whilst acknowledging this, the following advice suggests what should ideally be done to research possible schools for a child.

Read all the available information about each school, with the individual child in mind. Visit the school's website, read the prospectus and look at the results and the school's latest Ofsted report. Find out about the ethos of the school. If the child has a particular interest or aptitude, can the school cater for this – for example, is it especially strong in music, languages or sport, or does it have a thriving computer club or a school garden where the children can learn to grow flowers and vegetables? If the child has special educational needs or dyslexia, for example, a particularly strong special needs department or dyslexia unit could be a deciding factor.

Schools generally have a programme covering the social and emotional aspects of learning, or PHSE (personal, health, social and economic) education. Primary schools may have, for instance, "circle time", to promote social and emotional well-being among their pupils, covering subjects like friendship and bullying. All pupils should have access to pastoral care and support, as well as specialist services for those who are showing signs of problems. Ask the school about these, as they will clearly be very relevant to looked after children.

Go to any formal meetings for parents and carers of prospective pupils and ask questions. But don't rely solely on the prospectus and the formal meetings. Use informal sources too, if possible.

If the child's carers live locally, they may well have already formed an impression of the school from its reputation and/or what their friends or relatives have to say about it.

One of the best ways to find out about a school is to visit during an ordinary school day, rather than an open day or evening meeting. Most head teachers will be happy to allow this if you ask. So have a look around the school while it's working – along with the carers and the child himself, if possible.

On visits to the school, chat to pupils if you can. Ask them what they like or don't like about the school. Ask parents of current pupils, too, about their thoughts on the school and its strengths and weaknesses.

What is your impression of the school? How does it make you feel? How do you think it will make the child feel? The size of the school is important. A large school can be overwhelming. But many large schools function in smaller units, such as a lower school and an upper school, so the number of pupils on the school roll doesn't tell the full story. Some large schools manage to have a small school "feel" about them. Find out what you can about the pace and style of lessons and the content of the school curriculum – will it engage this child? What are the class sizes?

Look at the school from the child's perspective. If a child is timid, think about how the school corridors would feel to him when the students are changing classrooms between lessons. Are they noisy and daunting, with lots of children pushing and shoving?

This is where the work you have done on "learning the child" (see Tip 1) will be really helpful. Suppose you found out that the child has particular difficulties with, say, using a toilet when there are other people around, or that he has a problem like irritable bowel syndrome. And then you find out that a particular school you are considering for him has a rule that the toilets are locked except for an hour at lunchtime, and that students are not allowed to use them outside this time – which means students can't simply go to the toilet as and when they need to, and during the time the toilets are unlocked, they are always busy. The combination of the child's vulnerabilities and this particular school could be disastrous.

What does the child think?

Of course, you will need to ask the child himself which school he would like to go to. He may well have strong feelings for or against a particular school. Try to tease out why he feels this way. His attitude may be more to do with his peer group than with the school itself – for example, he may want to go to the same school as all his friends from primary school, or he may have negative feelings towards a particular school because of bad experiences with pupils from there.

You will need to consider whether, for example, going to the same school as his friends from primary school would be helpful. Would he benefit from retaining those friendships? Or are the relationships marked by conflict, bad behaviour or bullying?

Take him to visit the school or arrange for his foster carers to take him, to make sure he forms a realistic impression. Encourage the foster carers to look out for his reactions as they are shown around the school. Which displays interest him most? Which rooms does he not want to leave?

Jamie, 10, who has autism spectrum disorder, was taken to visit a secondary school where he might go at age 11. Looking round the school, his face was expressionless and he seemed uninterested. Then he came to a workshop where the technology teacher was building a car and explained that there was a weekly club for pupils who wanted to help work on the car. Without hesitation, Jamie announced: 'I'm coming here!' Once he started at the school he went to the car club every single week, and he formed a special bond with the technology teacher.

What do the foster carers think?

Foster carers who know the child well, and who are familiar with all the local schools, may be excellent judges of whether a particular school would suit him or not.

However, other considerations might come into play for them. They may be swayed by practical considerations such as the distance to the school. Foster families sometimes have quite strong views about the implications for their own children if a child they are looking after goes to the same school. In terms of practical arrangements, it can be easier for foster carers to manage having their own children and the looked after child at the same school. On the other hand, some carers feel that their own children need time away from the child(ren) they look after, and that it is easier for them if the foster child goes to a different school.

Choosing a different school for the looked after child (if he is in a long-term placement) could send the message that he is being treated less favourably than the carers' own children. The child needs to be consulted and the decision made with his best interests in mind. If it is decided to send him to a different school from that of the foster carer's children, or from his own preferred school, you or the foster carers should explain to him the reasons why you decided that particular school would suit him best.

Should a looked after child attend the same school as his birth siblings and other relatives?

If siblings are placed together then generally they should attend the same school, unless there are compelling reasons to believe they would do better apart.

Sometimes children can have several members of their extended family in the same school – some familial relationships are extremely complex and children may have uncles and aunts of school age as well as siblings and cousins attending the same school. Such situations can present a range of challenges, from arguments in the playground (between adults as well as children!) to safeguarding issues (when other children are in contact with adults who pose a risk to the child). When considering alternative schools for a particular child, you will want to consider the extended social network of the birth family, if they live locally, and whether this is likely to have a positive or negative impact for the child.

Getting a place for the child in your chosen school

A total of 16 per cent of children in care, compared to 10 per cent of their peers, go to the lowest-attaining primary schools, according to the DfE's new data tool for local authorities. At age 11, 10 per cent go on to secondaries where fewer than 35 per cent of pupils get five good GCSEs including maths and English, compared to six per cent of all children.

(Northen, 2011)

Getting a place in a popular school, in some places, is notoriously difficult. Getting a place for their child in the secondary school of their choice is something that preoccupies many parents and can cause a great deal of stress.

Looked after children are given the highest priority in the admissions criteria. So, in theory at least, they should be able to walk into the most sought-after school in town.

However, the education system is currently undergoing a period of change, with more and more schools becoming "academies" and new "free schools" being set up. These schools have greater autonomy and control over pupil entry than schools that remain under the control of the local authority. They are still required to give priority in admissions to looked after children. Outside the normal transition round, schools should admit looked after children even if the school is full.

On paper, then, looked after children should have the right to go to any school of their choice. In practice, however, this right risks being undermined – particularly if schools see looked after children as "problematic" or unlikely to do well, with results that could adversely affect the school's place in the league tables of results.

As The Adolescent and Children's Trust (TACT) points out:

> *...it is the actual day by day, school by school, informal process around school admissions that matters. These include: middle-class parents queue jumping; schools suggesting alternative schools would suit the child's needs better; weak corporate parenting; and foster carers lacking authority with school staff. This is not to suggest that such practices are endemic. The fact is we don't have firm data, just anecdotal evidence...*
>
> *(TACT, 2012)*

If you are convinced the child would benefit from being at a particular school and the school is reluctant to take him, you may need to advocate for the child and persevere in requesting a place. Contact the looked after children's education team at your local authority for advice. The virtual school head (see Tip 3) should also be able to help if you have a problem finding a place for a looked after child.

We owe it to looked after children to try to do the best we can for them, as we would for our own children. The only consideration should be which is the best school for the child. Other considerations, such as finance (the cost of transport), should not hold sway.

Going to a "good" school, with a strong work ethic and pastoral care, good behaviour and academic results and studying alongside children who are keen, interested and motivated to learn could transform the child's life chances.

TIP 6

Form a relationship with key school staff members

In the school

As the child's social worker, the key people for you to make links with are likely to be:

- the school's designated teacher for looked after children;

- in a primary school, the child's class teacher;

- in a secondary school, the teacher(s) responsible for pastoral care and academic achievement for the child's year group (whose job title may be head of year or head of achievement);

- the special educational needs co-ordinator (SENCO) or head of inclusion, for a child who has special educational needs;

● the teaching assistant or learning mentor, if there is one who has special responsibility for the child.

It can be difficult to know what job titles in schools actually mean and what the roles are, so don't be afraid to ask. You can say, for example, 'I'd like to speak to the person who can tell me about the curriculum the child will follow'.

Outside the school

There are other people who may be able to offer you advice and guidance on educational issues:

● the virtual school head or other staff from the virtual school (see Tip 3);

● the local authority's looked after children's education team (which may go by other names, e.g. looked after children education support team, or looked after children educational achievement team);

● the local authority's head of inclusion;

● education officers or education teams employed by some of the larger independent fostering providers;

● the child welfare officer;

● the child protection school liaison officer, employed by the local authority (where there are concerns about safeguarding in relation to the school).

Take an interest in the agendas of the teaching staff and the pressures affecting their work. Teaching and social work are both demanding jobs. There is sometimes a temptation for hard-pressed professionals to think about how tough their own job is and not to recognise the challenges facing those in other professions. But if professionals in different fields make the effort to abandon prejudices and find out more about each other's roles, they will reap the rewards in terms of deeper understanding and better relationships, which can only benefit the children they work with.

Communicate clearly and help the teaching staff to understand your perspective and the pressures and agendas that affect your work. Just as some social workers misunderstand teachers, equally some teachers find it hard to understand why, for example, a social worker might never manage to get to a school before 5pm to collect a child. Give some thought to the perceptions teachers might have about social workers – 'They're never there when you want them'; 'You see a different one every time'; or 'They cancel meetings at the last minute' – and try to explain why some of these things are unavoidable in social work. A little mutual respect, appreciation and understanding will go a long way towards building bridges with the teaching staff.

As both you and the teachers have full schedules, it can be difficult to find the time to develop these relationships. Try to plan ahead and identify times that are likely to be slightly less busy for both of you, and make the most of these opportunities. Lay the groundwork and then – if and when difficulties arise with the child – you will be better able to work together to find solutions.

Teachers are often subject to a stricter dress code than social workers, so some social workers tend to dress more casually. Some might attend a meeting at the school wearing jeans, for example, when everyone else is required to dress smartly. It's a good idea to be aware of how you might come across and make an effort to fit in with the culture of the school.

How you can help the designated teacher

Designated teachers were clear that comprehensive and up-to-date information on children was what they needed most in order to develop appropriate strategies and responses in school. They particularly wanted to know how to respond to distress and how to console a child who was looked after, in a way that would not evoke other experiences or compound difficulties. (Information that would not be included in a PEP). Designated teachers also wanted clear information about practical specifics – who to send reports to, invite to parents' evenings,

> *contact in an emergency, who could give permission*
> *for school trips and so on, as well as ongoing*
> *information about changes in circumstances.*
>
> *(Hayden, 2005)*

Tell the school about prohibited people

Make sure the school knows about anyone who is prohibited from having contact with the child, as well as what they should do and who they should notify if such a person turns up at the school or is seen waiting at the school gate.

Some children and young people will be at risk if their photograph or name(s) are circulated in the local community. So the school also needs to know about confidentiality requirements in relation to the child's history and any restrictions on, for example, photographing and otherwise identifying the child, in photographs of school events, the school magazine or reports in the local media. Discuss this with the designated teacher, and ensure the information is noted in the file that the school keeps on the child.

Check out who the key people are for the child

The child's class teacher (in a primary school) and head of year (in a secondary school) are obvious key people for the child. But you also need to ask the child which adults he likes or gets on with at school. These people may not be the ones you expect. For instance, looked after children often like the school library – a quiet place with corners where you can hide yourself away – so the school librarian may be someone they have got to know and connect with. Key people for the child in school may be the caretaker, a dinner lady, the school nurse, the office staff as well as (or instead of) a teacher, teaching assistant or learning mentor. Check regularly as the key people may change.

Reassure the child that although the designated teacher has a special responsibility for looking out for his interests, he will still be able to talk to the teacher with whom he gets on best or the person who has been identified as the "safe" person for him.

Who are the key people for the carers?

The relationships between the carers and key people in the school, such as the child's form teacher, are important. In some circumstances teaching assistants may take on the role of liaising with foster carers, for example, if the carers need to phone the school regularly to find out if the child has turned up for lessons or if he has been upset that day.

The designated teacher for looked after children (see Tip 3) is responsible for overseeing the child's progress, though he or she may delegate some responsibility for certain things to other people, such as the head of year, who will know the child better.

Again, check this regularly as it may change. See Tip 7 for advice on how to facilitate the link between the carers and the school.

Helping the teachers understand the child

Training for new teachers does not devote much time to attachment disorder or the effects on children of trauma, grief and loss (see Tip 1), so teachers may not have a good understanding of why some looked after children behave in the way they do. They may simply see a defiant and disruptive young person, not the damaged and hurt child within. One of the tasks of the designated teacher is to ensure that school staff learn about and understand the effects of trauma. You have an important role to play here too.

When an individual child is having behavioural issues in school and getting into trouble, you may need to work with school staff to help them understand where the child's difficulties come from and what strategies would work with him. This is a difficult task, demanding tact and diplomacy.

If the child has been getting into trouble, with incidents such as lashing out or walking out of school, the best policy may be to approach the head, the designated teacher or some other key person, to ask "what can we do about it?" This kind of approach has the best chance of success if you have already established good working relationships with the relevant people (see above).

As the child's social worker, you could suggest a team meeting of all the teachers who teach the child to talk about the effects of trauma on that child. It may work well to get someone from outside the school to facilitate a meeting to discuss what is happening and what strategies work best with him. You may wish to involve Virtual School staff to discuss how the school staff could work with the child to avoid exclusion or to improve his attendance and achievement. The SENCO might also be able to arrange for an educational psychologist to attend an after-school meeting to discuss individual children.

Training

You could also suggest some more general whole-school in-service training for staff on childhood trauma and how it can affect the way children function, behave and learn. The virtual school head teacher might be able to provide or arrange for such training. However, whoever gives the training will need to pitch it at the right level and take care not to patronise experienced teachers – some teachers will already have a good awareness that looked after children's challenging behaviour arises from their previous traumatic experiences, and what they are looking for is practical advice on how best to work with these children in their classrooms.

Bear in mind that teachers are asked to attend many after-school meetings. If you are asking them to attend a meeting about a child, or more general training, you will need to plan the content carefully to ensure the meeting is relevant, does not duplicate information they have already had and makes the best use of teachers' time.

Behaviour management

Often, teachers who are finding it difficult to manage a particular child's behaviour will say to the child's social worker, 'Tell me what to do'. However, when living or working with a traumatised child, the issue is not "what to do" but rather "how to be". A calm teacher who expresses his or her own feelings appropriately and stays in control of the emotional tone of the environment can create a feeling of safety and security, which will help to soothe the child's hyperarousal, fear or anger.

> *Adults need to practise "not startling the horses"*
> *when working with traumatised children, for*
> *children, like horses, are flight animals.*
> *Unfortunately many hyperaroused children appear*
> *anything but timid, and this leads people to treat*
> *them as frightening rather than frightened. The*
> *counter-intuitive technique is to assume with any*
> *challenging child that fear is a large part of the*
> *equation for the child, and at the same time to*
> *recognise that this will engender fear in the adult.*
> *So we must contain and manage our own fear,*
> *and soothe the terror of the child.*
>
> *(Cairns and Stanway, 2010)*

Of course, there may be times when a child or young person has to leave the classroom because their behaviour is unacceptably disruptive or because they are putting themselves or others at risk. The school will have a protocol for dealing with incidents like this, which will involve removing the child from the classroom and sending him to someone else, so that the teacher can continue to teach the rest of the class. In the case of a traumatised child, this protocol should ideally acknowledge and address the child's difficulties and should aim to help him to learn from the incident.

Kate Cairns and Chris Stanway (2010) suggest this nine-step structure for dealing with individual incidents of post-traumatic behaviour.

1. **Safety first.** If possible, move away from the location where the event was triggered. Try to be in a space the child regards as safe, and have an identified person, who is seen by the child as safe, to deal with the situation.

2. **Engaging.** While hyperaroused, the child will not hear or be able to process what is said to them. If necessary, agree to wait until later, when the child is calmer, to take the disciplinary process forward.

3. **Trusting and feeling.** When the child is able to hear and to process what you say, establish your trustworthiness and that you are not going to harm the child. Comment on their obvious strong feelings. Offer a narrative about the event that starts from feelings.

4. **Managing the self.** Invite the child to reflect on what happened and on what he was experiencing "inside" at the time. If the answer is "don't know", that tells us and the child something about his inner world.

5. **Managing feelings.** Acknowledge that strong feelings are uncomfortable and for this child can be overwhelming. Help the child to think of ways to prevent feeling overwhelmed. Explain that he always has choices, and explore how making choices might be more difficult for him than for others.

6. **Taking responsibility.** Now provide a narrative for what happened, being clear about what you know and what is hearsay. Check the child has heard and understood. Listen to what the child has to say and amend the narrative if necessary. Clearly state what the consequences will be, and reassure the child that these consequences will do them no harm. Be prepared to go back to providing safety if the child starts to become overwhelmed.

7. **Developing social awareness.** Help the child to think about the effects of the event on other people. Help the child to find strategies to reintegrate, positively, with the group.

8. **Developing reflectivity.** Encourage the child to reflect on what they have learned. Ask them to think of ways to regulate their behaviour next time, and to think about how they will know if they have improved. Comment positively on their courage in dealing with their difficulties, and check they have heard and understood this.

9. **Developing reciprocity.** Tell the child what you have learned by working with them on this. Thank them for anything you can thank them for.

If teachers have identified that this approach or any other strategy works well with the child in terms of behavioural support, this should be noted in the child's PEP (see Tip 3).

In-school support for children's and young people's emotional and mental well-being

As well as promoting children's well-being through PHSE lessons, anti-bullying initiatives and so on, some schools commission school-based mental health support for pupils with behavioural and emotional problems. This can be done in partnership with a range of different agencies. For example, the national charity The Place 2 Be (see *Useful Organisations*) is involved in 174 schools, providing one-to-one counselling sessions for individual children, lunchtime drop-in services for children and training and advice for teachers.

For head teachers who want to know more about providing school-based mental health support, you could recommend *Resilience and Results: How to improve the emotional and mental well-being of children and young people in your school*, a free resource produced by the Children and Young People's Mental Health Coalition (see *Useful Resources*).

Exclusion from school

Looked after children and young people are four times more likely to be permanently excluded from school than their peers (in England, 0.3 per cent were permanently excluded in 2010–11, compared to 0.07 per cent of all children). It goes without saying that permanent exclusion is extremely damaging for the child's life chances. It can also put the placement under a lot of pressure.

However, the statutory guidance for head teachers makes it clear that permanently excluding a looked after child or young person should be a last resort. Here are the relevant paragraphs:

> *22. As well as having disproportionately high rates of exclusion, there are certain groups of pupils with additional needs who are particularly vulnerable to the impacts of exclusion. This includes pupils with statements of special educational needs (SEN) and looked after children. Head teachers should, as far*

as possible, avoid excluding permanently any pupil with a statement of SEN or a looked after child.

23. Schools should engage proactively with parents in supporting the behaviour of pupils with additional needs. In relation to looked after children, schools should co-operate proactively with foster carers or children's home workers and the local authority that looks after the child.

24. Where a school has concerns about the behaviour, or risk of exclusion, of a child with additional needs, a pupil with a statement of SEN or a looked after child, it should, in partnership with others (including the local authority as necessary), consider what additional support or alternative placement may be required. This should involve assessing the suitability of provision for a pupil's SEN. Where a pupil has a statement of SEN, schools should consider requesting an early annual review or interim/emergency review.

48. It is important for schools to help minimise the disruption that exclusion can cause to an excluded pupil's education. Whilst the statutory duty on governing bodies or local authorities is to provide full-time education from the sixth day of an exclusion, there is an obvious benefit in starting this provision as soon as possible. In particular, in the case of a looked after child, schools and local authorities should work together to arrange alternative provision from the first day following the exclusion.

(Department for Education, 2012a, www.education.gov.uk/schools/ guidanceandadvice/g00210521/statutory-guidance-regs-2012)

Even temporary exclusions can add up to the child missing significant time in school, so you will want to work with the school to try to find other ways to manage the child's behaviour so that the use of this sanction is avoided if at all possible. If a child or young person you work with is having repeated exclusions or is at risk of permanent exclusion, seek help and advice from the looked after children's education team at your local authority or from the virtual head teacher.

New arrangements for school exclusion came into force in September 2012. Under the new arrangements, the process for challenging a school's decision to permanently exclude a pupil will change. The current system of independent appeal panels will be replaced by independent review panels. Where requested by the parent or person who has day-to-day parental responsibility for a looked after child, the local authority or academy trust will need to appoint an expert in special educational needs to advise the independent review panel. You may find yourself in the position of challenging a school's decision and supporting the child and his foster carers through the process. Again, if this happens you should seek advice from the looked after children's education team or virtual school.

Secondary traumatic stress in the child's network

It is well established that living with and working with traumatised children can sometimes cause "secondary traumatic stress" in foster carers and others. This is the stress that results from caring for or about someone who has been traumatised and, if not resolved, it can result in injuries similar to those produced by primary trauma. Over time, it can provoke reactions which change the thoughts and feelings of the adults involved, and damage their health.

Are people involved with the child at home and school starting to feel frustrated, demoralised and helpless and at a loss to know what to try next? Are people becoming tearful, irritable, or avoiding having to deal with the child? Are people failing to turn up to appointments? Are meetings about the child marked by disagreements and conflict? These can be signs of secondary stress in the network around the traumatised child. Losing a sense of appreciation of others in the child's network, with all their strengths and weaknesses, is another sign. Do people blame each other for what is going on?

People affected are often unaware of this developing disorder because of *avoidance*. Avoidance is a mechanism that protects us from becoming overwhelmed in the face of anger or other stress. Our mind closes down our consciousness of the thing that is threatening us. The condition then becomes self-perpetuating. The only protection against avoidant behaviour, then, is other people. The first step to containing and managing secondary trauma is knowledge. Getting together in a group – foster carers, teachers and social workers – to discuss the possibility of secondary stress can help everyone to reflect on what is going on with this child and how it might be affecting the way they themselves function.

> *It is vital to be knowledgeably self-aware, but this will fail in severe cases. It is therefore also vital to have others who understand the condition and will tell us if we are changing. We must also commit ourselves to hear and act on such information even though it feels inaccurate because of the changes in our functioning.*
>
> *...If the threat is a shared one, if many in the network are troubled by contact with the traumatised child, then there will be a shared avoidance that will be immensely powerful. We have to work very hard at staying open to preventing and stopping avoidance.*
>
> (Cairns and Stanway, 2010)

As the social worker, you may have an understanding of secondary traumatic stress which others in the network perhaps lack. So you may need to act as monitor for the well-being of others, including the foster carers and teachers. You may need to take the lead in looking at how the network is functioning and suggest the possibility of secondary traumatic stress – and remain open to the possibility that you yourself could be affected by it.

The adults in the network must be able to work together effectively if they are to meet the needs of the child. The factors that protect us from traumatic stress and enable us to recover are both personal and social. You may not be able to influence the personal factors that affect people's recovery, but you may be able to play a part in influencing at least some of the social factors. These social factors include strong but flexible networks, close confiding relationships, contact with people who understand trauma, and supportive supervision at work.

Understanding school funding

Social workers (and some newer teachers, too) can find it hard to understand the complexities and idiosyncrasies of school funding and which funding streams can be used for which purposes. Head teachers decide how and on what to spend the various grants and funds available to the school and can refuse requests from staff for funding for various activities. This can be demoralising and lead to school staff feeling that they can't do anything because "we don't have the funding". Creative solutions are called for. The designated teacher should advocate for every penny of the available funding to be spent on looked after children.

Sometimes the social worker may consider that a certain kind of support would help the child, such as one-to-one tuition – but the school may disagree. You need to respect the views of the teacher, as the education professional, as to what would be most helpful for the child. But at the same time, try to advocate for him and ask what extra support they feel would be most appropriate.

The programme of support should be designed to fit what the child needs, whether that is pastoral care, therapeutic help or one-to-one tuition. Don't fall into the trap of thinking it's absolutely vital for him to move up a level in terms of his SATs (standard assessment tests). However, if a child has missed a lot of school, then some extra one-to-one support to catch up on what he missed could well be helpful.

For a child who has moved to a new school, the highest priority would be to help him learn to trust people and to make new relationships. Once the child feels safe, settled and happy, improvements in school work will generally follow.

Schools, charities, looked after children's education teams and virtual heads may all be able to find ways of accessing funds for extra-curricular activities for looked after children, such as music tuition or sports coaching.

The Department for Education states that local authorities are working in a variety of ways to improve education outcomes for looked after children:

> *Local authorities that are effective in meeting their responsibilities demonstrate a strong commitment to providing additional resources to help all looked after children at risk of not reaching expected standards of attainment.*

and

> *Local authorities that are effective in promoting the educational achievement of their looked after children ensure that the offer of one-to-one tuition is available to all looked after children in Key Stage 2 and Year 7 who would benefit from this kind of additional support.*
>
> (Department for Education, 2012c)

The Pupil Premium

The Pupil Premium provides additional funding to schools for disadvantaged pupils. The Pupil Premium is a sum of money that is paid by the local authority to the school, for each child who is on free meals or who is looked after. The purpose of this funding is to close the gap in educational attainment between the most disadvantaged children and their peers from better-off families. All children who have been looked after for six months are eligible for the Pupil Premium.

The amount for the financial year 2012/13 was £600. It is expected to rise each year.

Some schools use the Pupil Premium to fund additional reading support and tuition in maths, literacy, speech and language, etc. However, the money is not ring-fenced and many schools have ended up using the money to plug holes in their budgets, rather than specifically allocating it to help poorer pupils.

Use of the Pupil Premium can be recorded on the PEP (see Tip 3).

Personal Education Allowance (abolished March 2011)

The Personal Education Allowance for looked after children was a sum of money which could be used to pay for extras which would promote the child's education through learning or other activities (e.g. extracurricular activities which would improve his social skills or build confidence). For instance, it could be used for one-to-one tuition, music lessons or equipment, computers or swimming lessons. Although it was abolished when the Pupil Premium was introduced, some local authorities have voted to continue paying the Personal Education Allowance. In authorities where the Personal Education Allowance is no longer given, the Pupil Premium often does not benefit individual looked after children in the same way because, as mentioned above, the funding is often swallowed up in the general school "pot".

TIP 7

Facilitate the links between the carers and the school

Find out who the key school staff will be for the carers

Make sure they are introduced to these people and feel confident to build relationships with them. The school should give the carers a named person to contact, such as the designated teacher, if they have concerns.

Ensure that carers are enabled and empowered to liaise with the school

You will need to make it clear to the carers (as well as the school) what they can, or cannot, take responsibility for in relation to the school. For example, it would normally be appropriate for the carers to sign the home–school agreement and attend parents' evenings.

You may need to make an agreement with the school that they will contact the carers immediately if the child does not turn up to school.

Delegated authority and permissions

Make sure the child's foster carers are clear about what they can and cannot give permission for the child to do. For instance, schools send permission slips home with children to be signed when they need permission for them to take part in activities such as school trips. Even if the responsibility for this rests with you as the child's social worker, you can delegate the task of signing permission slips to carers (see Tip 4). Tell the school who should be approached for permissions, and make sure this is noted in the child's PEP. As a general policy, it would be good practice for schools to reserve a place on the school trip for the looked after child and hold it open until the permission slip has been returned.

The Fostering Network set up a campaign in late 2012, highlighting the problems that arise for children when their foster carers are not allowed to make day-to-day decisions for them. Its report, *Like Everyone Else*, based on a survey of more than 1,000 foster carers across the UK, shows that many carers are still not allowed to make basic decisions.

● A third (30 per cent) cannot give permission for a child to stay over with a friend.

● One in five (17 per cent) cannot allow a child to go on a school trip.

Instead, foster carers reported that they have to ask permission from social workers, who are invariably required to seek the approval of a senior manager who may not know the child or their foster carer. This leads to unnecessary delay. As a result, fostered children often miss out on such activities, and in some cases can be bullied because the decision-making process sets them apart from other children.

Robert Tapsfield, Chief Executive of the Fostering Network, said:

> *We hear far too many examples of children missing out on the essential experiences of childhood because their foster carers are not allowed to make basic decisions. One girl wanted to go on a school trip, but because it took 16 weeks for the local authority to give permission, she couldn't go. That is ridiculous and the system has to change.*
>
> *(Fostering Network press release, 2012)*

Despite all four UK governments acknowledging the problem and issuing guidelines stating that more authority should be given to foster carers, three out of five (59 per cent of) foster carers said the level of authority they have has stayed the same or got worse over the last two years. The Fostering Network recommends that day-to-day decision making should be automatically delegated to foster carers unless otherwise specified, and that all four UK governments should run programmes to help local authorities to put this into practice.

Tapsfield said:

> *Foster carers are almost always best placed to make day-to-day decisions about the children they foster. Social workers need to be able to advise and support foster carers...There needs to be a change in culture within the system where instead of the social worker signing the form, it's the foster carer. Local authorities should see delegating more authority to foster carers as a positive step as it will free up time for social workers and reduce unnecessary bureaucracy.*

The child's care plan should set out the arrangements for delegated authority. It would be helpful for the carers to have some clear information that sets out who is responsible for what. Some responsibilities are held jointly. (See the checklist in Tip 4)

Ensure carers are enabled and empowered to take on the "parent" role

In recent years, there has been a change in emphasis regarding the role of foster carers. The 2011 Fostering Service Regulations (implemented from April 2012) make it clear that the foster carer is expected to do the things that a good *parent* would do. In fact, the Regulations specifically refer to foster carers as foster *parents*. Fostering services have taken this change on board, but some children's services have not yet made the shift towards seeing foster carers as taking on the role of parents rather than simply professional carers. Ensure that carers understand this change in their role and the positive impact it can have. They may need "permission" or encouragement to take it on, but it is important that they do.

The child or young person is likely to view both you, as the social worker, and the school staff as "professionals", and as the "corporate parent" you probably engage with the school in quite a formal way. So encourage the foster carers to engage with the school in the way that a caring parent would. This can be asking quite a lot of them, especially if they have a number of children placed with them or if you are maintaining the child in a school near his home and the foster carer lives a long way from the school. If visiting in person is difficult, the carer should still be able to keep in touch with the school and the teachers by phone.

The carers will be the ones who liaise with the school staff about most matters, such as how to motivate the child or young person to do his homework, behaviour issues, choosing subjects, asking if he can have a little help with keeping track of his assignments, and so on. The better their relationship with both the child and the teachers, the more effective they will be in getting him the support he needs.

Encourage carers to get involved with the school

Some carers may be prepared to volunteer in the child's school, for instance, by listening to children read or accompanying school trips. Some may even be prepared to take on a more formal role, such as joining the committee of the parent–teacher association or becoming a governor. You could suggest this, if they haven't already thought of it, and offer every encouragement – this kind of involvement demonstrates to the child that his foster carers are committed to his school and are prepared to give their time and energy to support it.

TIP 8

Ensure the child has information that makes sense to her

Provide meaningful information about the school

The school is likely to provide a lot of information for parents of prospective pupils, but if possible you also want to give the child information about a new school which is meaningful to her. Sometimes school pupils will have produced a child-friendly guide to their school – ask the school staff about this. If there is nothing supplied either online or on paper that is aimed at prospective pupils and written in "pupil-speak", perhaps you can encourage the school to produce something – perhaps you could talk to the parent–teacher association and suggest that they initiate a competition for different classes to produce posters or pieces of writing about the school. Other ways to help prepare a child include those listed below.

- On a visit to the school with the child, you could make a video as you walk around. Take her to the different parts of the school and help her orientate herself. Try to focus on things that appeal to this child and will make her feel positive about the school when she thinks about it afterwards, such as the dance studio, science lab, school vegetable garden or the climbing frame in the playground.

- Talk to the child about the school; remind her of what she saw and did and liked about it during her visit. Ask her what else she would like to know about it.

- Take photographs around the school and compile an album to give to the child.

- Draw a map of the school, with pictures to identify different buildings or parts of buildings, e.g. the gym, science lab, dining hall.

- Give the child some items associated with the school, e.g. a piece of school uniform, pen, a locker key, a library book for her to return when she starts there.

- If the school and the teacher are happy with this, you could take a photograph of the class teacher to give to the child.

- Alternatively, or in addition, you could record the sound of the class teacher's voice (he/she could record a short message to the child, saying 'I am looking forward to having you in my class'). Some children who have auditory hypersensitivity will find it helpful to hear the sound of the teacher's voice and get used to it before they start at the school.

- If there is a greetings ceremony that the school uses to welcome new pupils, such as a particular song in school assembly, you could record this and play it to the child.

- Is it possible to log in to the school's virtual learning environment? The school might be able to allow the child "guest access" before she actually joins the school, so she can start finding out more about the curriculum and homework.

- Introduce her to a child or children who are already at the school.

- Make sure she is kitted out with the school uniform and other equipment she needs.

You and/or the carers need to make sure the child understands the school rules and what the sanctions are for breaking them. Ensure she understands what the rules are, for example, about having mobile phones in school – otherwise, if she is asked on her first day to hand over her phone to the teacher, it could cause problems.

Ensure she understands that behaviour out of school, as well as in school, could lead to sanctions from the school.

When she gets her timetable, you or the carers should talk her through it and explain that she will have to go into different parts of the school for different lessons.

Listen to her views

At PEP meetings, the child or young person has the opportunity to have their say about how they feel about school and learning, and what is important to them. The PEP form which the child fills in will be designed to be easily accessible for children and young people to complete.

Celebrate successes

Celebrations are meaningful to a child, whether it's a favourite meal at home or a trip to a restaurant, a cake made by the foster carer to say "well done", an achievement assembly in school or a bigger event organised by the local authority or virtual school to reward and celebrate looked after children's efforts and achievements.

In 2011, Coventry City Council held a special awards ceremony for their looked after children. The prom-style ceremony celebrated the achievements of looked after children and young people in their school and home lives. Foster carers, social workers, teachers and other professionals nominated the children and young people, aged between five and 20 years old. Nominations ranged from "trying very hard at school" and being "an inspiration to others" to making "tremendous progress and showing drive and determination". More than 250 people attended the event, which was hosted by the Lord Mayor and a local BBC presenter.

TIP 9

Support the child through transitions

Recognise the significance of the transition for the child

Transitions are stressful for anyone. Many looked after children have great difficulties with managing stress, so transitions are particularly challenging for them. Transitions need to be planned carefully and children will need extra support at these times.

Many looked after children have to contend with too many transitions: from home to a foster placement or other kind of placement, and perhaps back home again (sometimes more than once, in a "revolving door" between home and care). They may go from one foster placement to another, or from a short-term placement to a long-term one, to live with a relative or to be adopted. A change of placement or return home from care might also mean moving to a different location and a new school. For many looked after children, school provides a kind of stability when everything else in their lives seems to be in constant flux. It is not hard to see why changing schools might feel particularly frightening and be hard to cope with.

Even when a child's foster placement is long-term and stable, he will still be faced with all the normal transitions of childhood and the teenage years: starting school, moving from infants to juniors, from primary to secondary school and then from secondary education into higher education or to work and eventual independence. It is well recognised in education circles that many children take a "step backwards" in terms of their educational achievements between leaving Year 6 and starting at secondary school in September at the beginning of Year 7. This is because leaving primary school and starting at secondary school represents a big transition. It is a challenge for all children – but even more so for those who are looked after.

A looked after child may struggle, more than most, to find their way around a new school, to get used to new routines, to understand what is expected of him and to form relationships with new people, both adults and other children. To a child with post-traumatic stress (as outlined in Tip 1), arriving at a new school must feel like landing in a foreign country. There is a sense of bewilderment, of not fitting in, not connecting with others or understanding what is expected of him. And, of course, for unaccompanied asylum-seeking children and young people who are in the care system, starting school in the UK is quite literally, as well as metaphorically, a foreign country.

Ensure information is transferred in good time

For transitions involving changes of school, it is crucial to ensure that information about the child is not lost, but reaches the right people in good time. The designated teacher has a key role in helping looked after children make a smooth transition to their new school or college, including making sure there are effective arrangements in place for the speedy transfer of information. Providing good quality information to a new school before the child starts makes it easier to get off on the right footing; the school will understand the child better and be able to deal with any emotional or behavioural problems effectively.

A new PEP is required whenever there is a change of school or change of placement.

Help the child to settle in a new school

Wherever possible, ensure that the child starts school at the "right" time, i.e. at the beginning of the school year rather than in the middle of a term. Starting a new school just a few days after everyone else marks a child out as "different" and makes him feel less secure, because all the other children will have found their way around and started to get to know each other, the teacher and the school routines.

You and his carers will need to spend time with him, preparing and reassuring him. The more the child knows in advance about his new school, the less anxious and confused he is likely to be. (See Tips 5 and 8, which deal with providing information to the child about the school.)

For children with post-traumatic stress disorder (PTSD), everyday tasks like finding their way around the school can be more difficult. Explain to the teacher that something as simple as moving a pot plant from one place to another, or a teacher's car that is parked in a different space from where it normally is, can leave a child confused if he has been using it as a "landmark" to orientate himself in the classroom or the playground.

Children with PTSD find it harder than their peers to remember things, to organise themselves and to make sense of their environment. Talk to the relevant people in the school so that they can offer extra support if necessary. Schools do a lot of integrative work to support children who do not speak English, such as a "buddy" scheme whereby another child befriends them to help them find their way around and so they are not left alone in the playground. You could use this analogy to try to help teachers see why a looked after child who has emotional, behavioural and social difficulties would benefit from similar support to integrate into his new school and peer group.

Explain that the child is likely to feel agitated and may find it difficult to calm himself down. Help the teachers to understand the kind of things that the child is likely to struggle with.

- When the child or young person first starts in a new school, they may cope better if their whole day is structured for them. Unstructured time in the playground can be particularly hard to manage and may leave them floundering. Ask the teacher if it's possible to have activities to keep the child occupied during "free" time.

- Can the teacher suggest a "safe place" – a quiet spot where the child will be allowed to withdraw from the fray, when it all gets too stressful for him?

- Is there a "safe person" that the child feels comfortable with, such as the teaching assistant, school librarian or lunchtime superviser, who could keep him under his or her wing until the child feels more secure?

- Encourage the teacher to think of little measures to put in place to help the child, e.g. a "buddy" system; labelling rooms and coat-pegs; and giving the child five minutes' notice before he will have to finish an activity or move to a different lesson.

- An anxious child might find it helpful to take into school with him something that will make him feel more secure, such as a small teddy. If he is attached to the foster carer, he might want to take something he associates with them, e.g. a special pen or a small scarf which smells of the scent she uses. For some children, the things that will comfort them might be more quirky, like a toy belonging to the family dog. The better you know the child, the more you are likely to be able to come up with ideas to help him cope with transitions.

- A child who has been sexually or physically abused may be extremely reluctant to get changed for PE or games, so you will need to warn the teacher about this in advance and discuss how best to manage it.

Help the child prepare for questions

Children and young people usually hate to be "different" or to stand out from their peers in any way. Starting at a new school means they have to negotiate this all over again with a new peer group. Their new classmates may be curious about, for instance, why they are of a different ethnicity from their carers, why they are joining the school in the middle of the school year, why they call their carers by their first names instead of "mum and dad", and why they have to do certain things differently, e.g. leave lessons for meetings with a social worker, or get special permissions for certain activities. It will help the child if you and/or his carers could talk about these issues with him and work out how much he should tell people about his background and his situation, and how he should phrase it. Make it clear that if other children are asking questions, he doesn't have to give any more information than he feels comfortable with.

It is a good idea to discuss with the child's teachers any subjects or topics that are likely to be particularly sensitive or distressing for him – see Tip 6.

Prepare him for travelling independently

For an older child who is starting at secondary school or transferring to a sixth-form college and who is not used to travelling independently, it might be a good idea to encourage the carers to take the new journey with him once or twice (either accompanying him or maintaining a discreet distance behind him), to familiarise him with the route. If he is not used to travelling by public transport, they can have a couple of trial runs to ensure he knows where to get off the bus.

Boost his confidence

Starting at sixth-form college can be daunting for a young person. He may be desperate to be accepted by the new peer group. Think creatively about any ways you and the carers can boost his confidence – for example, a stylish new haircut and some new clothes or trainers can go a long way to making a young person walk tall and feel good about themselves.

Avoid placing extra stress on the child at times of transition

Young people need to be assured of the maximum possible stability in their home circumstances, particularly during exams and in the run-up to them.

> *A major problem for some young people was that their social workers hadn't planned things enough to **avoid major changes happening at the same time as school or college exams,** when the young person was less likely to be able to cope with them, or might do badly in their exams because other major changes were being made to happen in their lives:*
>
> *'They kept calling me during my final A-level exams, telling me I had to move out and had to fill in an application form. This caused me a lot of upheaval and they shouldn't have been bothering me around this stressful time.'*
>
> *(Office of the Children's Rights Director for England, 2006)*

Moving on

Schools themselves are facing a number of transitions, including introducing a new examination, the English Baccalaureate Certificate (EBC), to replace GCSEs, and the raising of the school leaving age.

From the summer of 2013, young people must stay in education or training (part-time in some cases) until the end of the academic year in which they reach their 17th birthday. From 2015, the leaving age will be raised to the end of the academic year in which they reach their 18th birthday.

Young people will need to decide what to do with the extra two years of education after the EBC, and whether to pursue academic or technical/vocational subjects. They may choose to do A-levels or a range of other qualifications, e.g. BTECs and City and Guilds qualifications.

If a looked after child is still in education, he is entitled to financial help in the form of the 16–19 Bursary.

The Pathway Plan

The Pathway Plan, which includes the care plan, is drawn up for a looked after young person when they are no longer in compulsory education, in order to prepare them for the transition to adulthood, which could include offering them the support necessary to move to greater independence when they feel ready. The child's social worker should draft the Pathway Plan before any referral for leaving care support, although he or she may wish to seek the views of the authority's leaving care service about how the young person's needs might be best supported in future.

This document is separate from the Personal Education Plan, Individual Education Plan and Pastoral Support Plan. You will need to arrange a meeting at the appropriate time to ensure the smooth transition of information from the PEP into the Pathway Plan.

Leaving care – what are the responsibilities of "corporate parents" to young people who want to study?

Local authorities are legally required to pay a Higher Education Bursary. Section 23C of the Children Act 1989 requires a local authority to pay a Higher Education Bursary to "former relevant children" who pursue a course in higher education in accordance with their pathway plan. (See *The Children Act 1989 (Higher Education Bursary)(England) Regulations 2009*.)

Student Finance England does not count this money or support when calculating entitlement for student finance.

For how long do "corporate parents" need to support a looked after young person in their education? For many young people in care, their educational journey is not smooth and it does not end at 16 or even 18. They may have some years out of education and then, later, when they are more mature and settled, wish to return to education and make up for what they missed.

There was a change in the law from April 2011 which means that care leavers up to the age of 25 who tell their local authority that they have returned, or want to return, to education or training, are entitled to be supported. Not everyone is aware of this. Make sure young people leaving care understand that they are entitled to this support if they want to return to education or training at a later date.

A local authority must provide "former relevant children" who take up further education or training with financial assistance and support from a personal adviser up to (and even beyond) the age of 25.

The National Care Advisory Service has produced a booklet for young people who have left care, called *Support for Young People aged 21 to 25 with Education and Training*. This clarifies the legislation and includes tips on how to get the support they need and how to ensure everyone knows about the duty on local authorities (see *Useful Resources*).

> *I was in care, permanently excluded from education at 14, and written off by the care system. My journey has been long and far from smooth, but, now aged 36 and completing my PhD, I am a clear example of why care leaver support must be extended. Policymakers fail to "think stage not age" when deciding when a care leaver no longer needs support. The whole system is obsessed with outcomes at 16 or 19.*
>
> *(Kerr, 2012)*

Going to university – or not?

Currently only around seven per cent of looked after teenagers make it to university, compared with 40 per cent of their peers. There are many more who have the potential but who, for many reasons, are performing below their capability at school. Others will be capable of getting the necessary grades but may feel that university is not for them. The attitudes of people they talk to about this – teachers, foster carers, and you as their social worker – will be crucial in either encouraging or discouraging their aspirations.

> *The idea that university is a desirable and attainable goal should be planted as early as possible.*
>
> *(Jackson, 2005)*

If a looked after young person is academically able and keen to go on to higher education, there should be nothing to stand in his way.

If the young person wants to go to university and the teachers at his school or sixth-form college believe this is a realistic aspiration, he will need to find out in advance which subjects at AS and A-level would give him the best chance of getting a place on his chosen university course.

University means a lot more freedom but also demands self-discipline, because the emphasis in many subjects is on independent study. Students need to organise their own time and be disciplined about focusing on work. How does the young person feel about this? What role will his birth relatives play? If a young person is thinking of applying for a place at university, and he is likely to be in contact with birth relatives or even returning to them, will they support his aspirations or undermine them and try to change his mind? It might be worth talking this through with him well before anything untoward happens.

If the foster carers and their own children did not go to university, they may not be able to see the point of higher education, or they may be concerned at the thought of the young person taking on a student loan. If you sense that their attitudes or doubts might deter the young person from considering university, you may need to step in with some facts to correct any misconceptions about the financial implications (see below). And the jobs market may be bleak, but graduates are faring better than most.

Again, the key question professionals should ask themselves is: 'What would I want for my own children?'

Aside from all other considerations, going to university also affords a young person three years in which to mature and develop independence in a rather more caring and protected environment than if he were to simply leave care and have to find a job and accommodation out in the "real world". Clearly, this could be particularly helpful for some young people who have grown up in care.

Leaving their foster home to move to a university in another town will probably represent one of the biggest transitions the young person has made. If he has become attached to the foster carers, it separates him from his attachment figures, which will be difficult for some. It also presents a set of exciting new challenges – getting to know a completely different place, living independently for the first time, budgeting, making a new set of friends and of course studying a subject they like in more depth and in a different way. This new start is likely to be full of optimism and opportunity for those young people who have the ability and confidence to take advantage of it.

University: the money facts

Many universities raised their fees to the maximum of £9,000 for the academic year 2012/13. This is paid by the Government direct to the university in the form of a tuition fee loan. The student does not have to repay the loan until they have graduated and are earning over £24,000. Then they make repayments on a sliding scale, with interest, over their working life. Any remaining debt is written off after 30 years.

If young people in care do not return to their parents on leaving care, they are considered "independent" and their parental income is not taken into account, so (on top of the Higher Education Bursary from the local authority) they will receive the maximum maintenance grant (which does not have to be repaid) and maintenance loan. The maintenance loan (to cover part of a student's living costs) is paid direct into the student's bank account and is repayable under the same conditions as the loan for tuition fees.

National scholarships are also available to students with a family income of £25,000 or less, which waive the first year of tuition fees. Care leavers will have priority for these scholarships. The young person should find out what support is offered at the various universities they are interested in. For example, the University of Exeter offers financial support to students who have been in care in the form of a full fee waiver for UK undergraduates and PGCE students starting in 2013, and a Care Leavers' Bursary. And many universities offer extra help to care leavers in the way of hardship funds and bursaries. Make sure any application for a loan is submitted in good time, because if it is late the money may not be in place for when the young person starts university.

There is a lot of uncertainty among young people about how much university is likely to cost and what support is available for them. You may need to talk the young person through this.

What other help do care leavers need when they go to university?

Some universities run special events for care leavers to encourage them to aspire to go to university, to help them find out about university life and explain the application process. You could find out whether there are any such events in your region and encourage the young person to attend. This will involve the local authority in funding his transport costs, just as a caring parent would.

Some local authorities arrange with the foster carers to keep the young person's placement open so that he has a home to come back to during the university holidays for the first year or even beyond. Clearly, if this can be done it makes a huge difference to young students who are not ready for complete independence from the foster family. It means a student's experience of university life is much more similar to that of his peers, for example, he is not left alone in his accommodation during the Christmas vacations.

A number of universities undertake to make available year-round accommodation for care leavers who want it or who have no other option.

The charity Buttle UK has developed a "quality mark" scheme for colleges and universities which demonstrate a commitment to supporting care leavers (see www.buttleuk.org).

Preparing for university

As well as clear information about financial support, young people who hope to go to university will need help with other things such as:

- researching and choosing a course and a university – to find out more about a particular course, as well as reading the official prospectus, he can contact current students through websites like the Student Room or the university's Facebook page;

- attending open days at the universities he is interested in – it's important that he sees a place for himself and gets a feel for it. For example, he may prefer a campus university to one that is located within a city;

- completing the UCAS application form and writing a "personal statement";

- preparing for and attending university interviews (e.g. researching the course by contacting students already on the course; doing "wider reading" around his subject; and finding someone to help him prepare by giving mock interviews). You may not know much about the young person's academic subject, but you can probably give him good advice about expressing himself clearly and projecting the right attitude and body language during interviews.

Hampshire County Council has worked in partnership with the University of Winchester to offer a three-day residential visit at the university for young people in care aged 14–17. The aim is to give young people from a care background an opportunity to experience university life, such as taking part in activities, engaging with current students and living in halls of residence. It is also a way of promoting the higher education opportunities open to them.

(Local Government Association, 2012)

Studying for exams

The final hurdle for the young person, of course, is getting the required grades in his A-levels. Exams are a particularly stressful time for a young person if a university place hinges on the results. Foster carers will need to help keep him on track with academic work and help him to cope with the stress. With luck, they will know him well enough and have a good enough relationship to understand what will work best for him. Worrying about exams can manifest itself in different ways, including anxiety, sleepless nights, tearfulness, irritability or sudden rages. Some may "switch off" and decide they can't do it after all.

Some young people will be self-motivated and self-disciplined when it comes to studying and revision, while others may need varying degrees of chivvying, encouragement and incentives to get them to put in the work. Foster carers, if they have a good relationship with the young person, may be able to help him develop his study skills. Ensure that the young person has a suitable place to study in the foster home, with a desk and a computer. Ask him if there any barriers to studying, for example, are the younger children in the household interrupting him while he is working?

Carers may have had a rule like "no music while you are doing your homework" – this is the time to start to relax the rules and let the young person work out for themselves what they find helpful or not. Some young people find it easier to concentrate on their work when they have music on in the background.

Some young people will need strategies to help them to focus and concentrate on studying and revising for sustained periods; they may find it hard to resist the temptations of Facebook, computer games and partying. If they admit that they are constantly being distracted by checking Facebook, for example, here is a tip that might help. Suggest they change their password to something they can't remember easily – a long string of unrelated letters and numbers – and write it down on a piece of paper which they then give to the foster carers. The foster carers agree to give them the password at an agreed time, e.g. when they have been working solidly for two hours, or in three days' time when they have finished their essay. (Obviously, this only works for young people who admit they have a problem, who trust their foster carers and who actively want to help themselves!)

Other young people have the opposite problem: they may put themselves under pressure by worrying about their exams, studying non-stop and working themselves up into a panic before exam day. They may need some encouragement to stop working at a certain time, switch off and relax a bit before bedtime so that they are more likely to sleep. It goes without saying that sufficient sleep, eating properly (rather than junk food and strong coffee), some rest and relaxation, and some exercise will help keep them on an even keel during the stress of the run-up to exams.

What other support should "corporate parents" give to university students?

The group thought that Corporate Parent boards in local authorities need to look closely at how their authorities help those in their care, or leaving their care, in their education – and how they tell them what help and financial support is there for them. Having "corporate parents" can be very different from having parents who will push for you and find things out for you.

(Office of the Children's Rights Director for England, 2012)

Apart from financial support, there are many other ways "real" parents support young people during their university careers. In an Institute of Education report, titled *Going to University from Care*, the following recommendations were made in relation to the support that local authorities, in their role as "corporate parents", should provide:

- *Ensure that a known person accompanies the student to university at the start of the year to provide transport and help with settling in.*

- *Have a clear policy on help for those who get into financial difficulties, especially when, for whatever reason, they are unable to meet basic needs.*

- *A designated representative must keep in regular touch with the student and not rely on them to make contact.*

- *This person should keep track of the student's performance in end-of-year assessments and examinations and give encouragement and support as appropriate.*

- *The local authority should be proud of the young person's achievement and mark it by ensuring that someone of the student's choice can attend the degree ceremony. The usual expenses should be met, including travel costs, hire of academic dress, photographs and a celebratory meal.*

(Jackson, 2005)

TIP 10

Assess the network for areas of positive impact

Is there anyone in the child's family who is able and willing to support the child in their education?

If you dig deep enough, you may be able to find people in the child's extended birth family who can be a positive influence on his education. Is there an older sibling who has left home, or perhaps an aunt or uncle, who would take an interest and encourage the child? Social workers often forget to look for the "escapees" from a dysfunctional family, but if you look hard enough there may be someone. Their involvement needn't mean a great deal of input, for example, you could simply tell the child that you are going to make sure Auntie sees his school report because she likes to know that he is doing well. It's someone who can hold the "positive narrative" for the child – see Tip 1.

Of course, you need to think carefully about the impact of this contact with the relative and who it might potentially bring into the child's network.

The child's parents may need to be involved in some decisions, and indeed may have a legal right to be involved.

Is there anyone in the wider network of the foster family who could support the child's education?

Also look at the resources of the foster care network, and cast your net wide – consider the foster carers' own parents, older birth children or previous foster children of the carers, as well as respite carers, previous foster carers the child is still in contact with, close family friends of the foster carers, and so on. There may be someone who can play an active role in encouraging and supporting the child's education. Or there may be a friend or relative who can be a positive role model for going to university, in spite of a difficult start, or who has a particular career or job that the child or young person aspires to.

Is there any other potential education champion for the child?

Apart from the obvious people such as the child's teachers, other school staff and the local education authority's looked after children education team and/or virtual school, can you think of any other potential education champions for this child? An adult who takes an interest in the child's or young person's progress and wants him to do well – even if this person does not have a specific "educational" role – can help to motivate him and keep him on track. Here are a few suggestions:

- the education team from the independent fostering agency, if the foster carers work with such an agency;

- an independent visitor;

- a mentor or counsellor (e.g. from a voluntary organisation);

- a sports coach, dance teacher or music tutor;

- a youth leader, e.g. if child belongs to the Brownies, Scouts or another youth organisation;

- voluntary organisations that can champion the child in relation to any specific needs, e.g. the Autism Society if he is on the autistic spectrum; the British Dyslexia Association if he has dyslexia;

- local councillors (the council as a whole is the corporate parent and councillors have a key role in deciding policies that affect looked after children's lives);

- someone from the therapy service, if the child is having therapy;

- someone from the child's church or other faith community;

- someone whom the young person has got to know during the course of work experience or volunteering with a charity or voluntary organisation, who takes an interest in their progress;

- organisations that advocate for children in care, or leaving care.

The role of therapeutic support

Sometimes you will need to refer a child to the Child and Adolescent Mental Health Service (CAMHS) for therapeutic help. There are also charities and voluntary organisations such as The Place 2 Be (see *Useful Organisations*), which offer counselling in schools from volunteers (many of whom are on clinical placements). If the child does not meet the threshold for a CAMHS referral but you think he would benefit from some individual support, talk to the designated teacher or head teacher about the possibility of a referral for school-based counselling.

Blue Smile is one such charity, offering counselling and mentoring to troubled children in Cambridgeshire schools (see *Useful Organisations*).

The kind of cases we see involve, for example, a child like "Jake" who faced neglect and emotional abuse as a child, never sure what would happen when his mother's changing partners came into the home. As a result, he became very wary of adults, but at the same time had to take on an adult role in making sure his two younger siblings were fed and protected from some of the violence.

He and his siblings were taken into care when Jake was six and, despite the deficits of his previous home life, he experienced this as a huge loss, which he was utterly powerless to prevent. By this time, he was also a self-sufficient and aggressive child, stealing and stockpiling food and others' toys in a world he felt to be chaotic and uncaring.

He was placed in long-term foster care with an experienced family who understood the reasons for his behaviours, but who began to struggle with his relentless rejections and assaults. From his point of view, he had been fostered alone, so felt he had lost his role as "family protector" and might also face further random losses. Time and again, he ran away with some thought in his head that he could pull his original family back together.

At school, he was understandably distracted and disruptive, so was eventually referred to Blue Smile for therapeutic support. Jake found one-to-one help from a therapist very hard at first, rubbishing what they did together and rejecting any positive exchanges. He seemed to be making sure that, for once, he would take charge of the ending of a relationship in his life.

However, over time, he began to trust his therapist and to enjoy his time with her. Through this relationship, he learned that adults could be caring and interested, that good feelings could be experienced in another's company and that life was not simply one long fight. He finally allowed himself to settle into his foster family, who have decided they want to keep him long term.

Jake's therapy has now finished and he is thriving in school, working well and making new and good friends.

(Blue Smile provided this composite case based on some of the experiences of a wide variety of children and young people it has supported.)

Out of school hours learning

Local sports, cultural and leisure organisations, clubs, classes and activities are all part of the wider network that can potentially offer opportunities that will enhance the lives of children in care.

Sarah, 13, has been in the same placement since she came into care (three years earlier). In the beginning, the foster carers and social worker had to work hard just to settle her into normal family life. Sarah had not attended school for many months and was frightened by the prospect. She had been the main carer for her three young brothers, and it was hard for her to give up that role and accept that she could allow adults to care for her. She had no idea about routines, had no appropriate clothing for her age, and had never had a bedroom of her own.

Sarah's social worker attended the launch of the Taking Part Out of School Hours Learning project. At this time Sarah was not involved in any extra-curricular activities, but she was attending school, loved shopping for clothes, and had helped her foster carers decorate her bedroom. Sarah was not keen on the idea of joining in activities, but with encouragement she went to modern dance classes. She not only loved it, but found out that she had natural rhythm and picked up new dances quickly. Sarah is now doing jazz dance and has discovered that she is very good at it.

Sarah's social worker said that she had no confidence when she first came into care and few social skills but, through dance, she has found something that she is good at and is enjoying the "positives" she receives from her carers. She has begun to think about taking up a musical instrument, and she has already been told: 'Decide on what instrument you want to play and lessons will be arranged'.

(ContinYou, 2005)

Make sure that the child is accessing all the financial support he is entitled to in order to support his educational and extra-curricular activities, including the cost of transport and equipment. Apart from the local authority's financial support, the school, the looked after children's education support team, the virtual school and other organisations may be able to help him access grants to support certain extra-curricular activities.

The Care Leavers' Foundation Trust Fund (see *Useful Organisations)* provides small grants for care leavers over 20 years old to support their education, training and employment needs, among other things.

Gifted or talented?

If a young person in your care is particularly gifted or talented, either academically or in music, sport or some other area, hopefully the school will already have identified this. However, if you have reason to believe the young person may be gifted or talented and that this has not yet been identified, talk to the teacher at the school who is responsible for gifted and talented pupils. If the young person is considered suitable, he should be offered a range of stimulating extra educational activities and opportunities that will challenge him and keep him engaged.

There are educational organisations which offer summer schools and longer-term programmes of educational activities, courses and mentoring for certain gifted and talented young people, particularly those from disadvantaged backgrounds, in order to help maximise their potential and increase their chances of getting into university. Check out the Sutton Trust (www.suttontrust.com) and the Villiers Park Educational Trust (www.villierspark.org.uk), for example (also see *Useful Organisations).*

As a "corporate parent", can the local authority provide work experience and other opportunities for looked after young people?

When the time comes for pupils to go on work experience, the local authority may be able to offer opportunities for the children in its care, like the example given below.

Bolton Metropolitan Borough Council's Looked After Supported Employment (LASE) Scheme provides paid work experience for "looked after" young people, usually aged between 16 and 19. It is an opportunity for them to gain new and positive experiences within a functional workplace environment. Most young people on LASE enrol on an accredited qualification, which in many cases can take up to 12 months to complete. The scheme supports the pathway planning work of Bolton's Post-16 social work team. Council departments have responded impressively to their "corporate parenting" role by offering looked after young people a range of work experience opportunities.

(Local Government Association, 2012)

Conclusion

Education is one of the most powerful ways of changing a life.

> *I am not interested in the past. I am interested in the future, for that is where I expect to spend the rest of my life.*
>
> *(Charles F Kettering, American inventor and engineer)*

Looked after children have troubled pasts, and many continue to face more stress and more challenges than most other children. The child or young person may be asking, by his words and actions, 'What's the point of going to school?' Social workers can demonstrate to looked after children and young people, by their own words and actions, that their education is important. They can show that it matters to them that the child is happy and doing as well as he can at school. If you do whatever you can to make the child's life as stable and secure as possible, if you can help him develop a feeling of self-worth, if you can give him hope for the future, those are the conditions in which he will want to learn.

The Charter for Care Leavers is a set of "principles and promises" which care leavers urge local authorities to use when they make decisions about young people's lives. It was developed in 2012 by the Department for Education and The Careleavers Foundation. The words below, part of the Charter, were written in relation to care leavers. But when we think of the support social workers can give to the education of children in care, this commitment is equally valid for looked after children and young people of any age:

> *We will value your strengths, gifts and talents and encourage your aspirations. We will hold a belief in your potential and a vision for your future even if you have lost sight of these yourself. We will help you push aside limiting barriers and encourage and support you to pursue your goals in whatever ways we can. We will believe in you, celebrate you and affirm you.*
>
> *(Department for Education and The Careleavers Foundation, 2012)*

References

All-Party Parliamentary Group for Looked After Children and Care Leavers (2012) *Education Matters in Care: A report by the independent cross-party inquiry into the educational attainment of looked after children in England*, London: All-Party Parliamentary Group for Looked After Children and Care Leavers

Allan C (2012) 'The most powerful stories are in our heads', *The Guardian (Society),* 3.10.12

Bath Spa University and Bath and North East Somerset Council (2012) *In Care In School* materials, Bath: Bath Spa University and Bath and North East Somerset In Care Council

Cairns K and Fursland E (2007) *Trauma and Recovery: A training programme*, London: BAAF

Cairns K and Stanway C (2010) *Learn the Child: Helping looked after children to learn, A good practice guide for social workers, carers and teachers*, London: BAAF

Centre Forum (2011) *Parenting Matters: Early years and social mobility*, London: Centre Forum

Chater D and Le Grand J (2006) *Looked After or Overlooked? Good parenting and school choice for looked after children*, London: The Social Market Foundation

ContinYou (2005) *Taking Part: Making out-of-school-hours learning happen for children in care*, London: ContinYou, available at: www.continyou.org.uk/files/taking-part.pdf (accessed 22.11.12)

Daniel B and Wassell S (2002) *The School Years: Assessing and promoting resilience in vulnerable children 2*, London: Jessica Kingsley Publishers

Department for Children, Schools and Families (2010a) *Promoting the Educational Achievement of Looked After Children: Statutory guidance for local authorities*, London: Department for Children, Schools and Families

Department for Children, Schools and Families (2010b) *Guidance on Looked After Children with Special Educational Needs Placed out of Authority*, London: Department for Children, Schools and Families, available at: www.teachernet.gov.uk/wholeschool/sen/

Department for Education (2012) *Statistical First Release: Outcomes for children looked after by local authorities in England as at 31 March 2012*, London: DfE

Department for Education (2012a) *Statutory Guidance and Regulations on Exclusion*, London: Department for Education, available at: www.education.gov.uk/schools/guidanceandadvice/g00210521/statuto ry-guidance-regs-2012

Department for Education (2012b) *Support and Aspiration: A new approach to special educational needs and disability*, London: Department for Education, available at: www.education.gov.uk/ publications/standard/publicationDetail/Page1/CM%208027#download ableparts

Department for Education (2012c) *The Role of Local Authorities in the Education of Looked After Children: Statutory duties on local authorities as corporate parents*, available at: www.education.gov.uk/ childrenandyoungpeople/families/childrenincare/education/a00208589/ role-of-local-authorities (accessed 22.11.12)

Department for Education and The Careleavers' Foundation (2012) *The Careleavers' Charter*, available at: http://resources.leavingcare.org/ uploads/455819f3bb6e038ddf750b2ec2a6b245.pdf

Family and Parenting Institute (2012) *Families on the Front Line? Local spending on children's services in austerity*, London: FPI

Fostering Network (2012) *Care System Denying Fostered Children*

Proper Experience of Childhood, Charity Warns, press release, 25 October, available at: www.fostering.net/media/2012/care-system-denying-fostered-children-proper-experience-childhood-charity-warns

Fursland E (2011) *Foster Care and Social Networking: A guide for social workers and foster carers*, London: BAAF

Gutman L and Vorhaus J (2012) *The Impact of Pupil Behaviour and Wellbeing on Educational Outcomes*, London: Department for Education Research Brief (DFE-RB254), available at: www.education.gov.uk/publications/eOrderingDownload/DFE-RB253.pdf

Harris J (2012) 'Omnishambles strikes again – and this time it's personal', *The Guardian*, 29.10.12

Hayden C (2005) 'More than a piece of paper? Personal Education Plans and looked after children in England', *Child & Family Social Work*, 10:4, pp. 343–352

IPSEA (Independent Parental Special Education Advice) Press release, 10.10.12, available at: www.ipsea.org.uk/AssetLibrary/News/IPSEA%20Press%20Release%20on%20draft%20provisions.pdf (accessed 7.12.12)

Jackson S (2005) *Going to University from Care* (Appendix 1, 'The path from care to graduation'), London: Institute of Education

Kellaway K (2010) 'Mohammad Razai: from child Afghan asylum seeker to Cambridge undergraduate', *The Observer*, 20.6.10

Kerr M (2012) 'Care leavers' charter must guarantee more support for young people', *The Guardian*, 30.10.12

Local Government Association (2012) *Corporate Parenting Resource Pack,* available at: www.local.gov.uk/c/document_library

Northen S (2011) 'Nobody's priority?', *The Guardian*, 20.9.11

Office of the Children's Rights Director for England (2006) *About Social Workers: A children's views report*, available at: www.rights4me.org

Office of the Children's Rights Director for England (2012) *The Minister's Discussion Group for Young People on Education for Children in Care: A children's views report*, available at: www.rights4me.org

Pallett C, Simmonds J and Warman A (2010) *Supporting Children's Learning: A training programme for foster carers*, London: BAAF

Ryan M (2012) *Relationships Matter for Looked After Young People: A guide for managers and commissioners*, London: NCB

Stothart C (2011) *How Fostering Education is Improving the Education of Looked After Children*, available at: www.communitycare.co.uk/articles/06/01/2011/116056/how-fostering-education-is-improving-the-reading-of-looked-after-children.htm (accessed 26.11.12)

TACT (2012) *In School and Out of School: Admissions, exclusion and children in care*, available at: www.tactcare.org.uk/news.php?type=4&id=264 (accessed 1.11.12)

Thomas N, in foreword to *In Care In School*, Bath: Bath Spa University

Useful organisations

British Association for Adoption and Fostering (BAAF)
Leading UK-wide membership organisation for all those concerned with adoption, fostering and childcare issues, with offices around the UK.
Saffron House
6–10 Kirby Street
London EC1N 8TS
Tel: 020 7421 2600
www.baaf.org.uk

Blue Smile
A Cambridgeshire charity offering school-based counselling and mentoring.
67 Grange Road
Cambridge CB3 9AA
Tel: 01223 872619
www.bluesmileproject.org

Buttle UK
Provides practical support, including financial grants, for children and young people living in poverty. Buttle UK has offices throughout the UK.
Audley House
13 Palace Street
London SW1E 5HX
Tel: 020 7828 7311
www.buttleuk.org

The Care Leavers' Foundation
Provides information, advice and financial support to care leavers aged 18–29.
PO Box 202
Bala LL23 7ZB
Tel: 01678 540 598
www.thecareleaversfoundation.org

Child Exploitation and Online Protection Centre (CEOP)
A police organisation which seeks to eradicate the sexual abuse of children, including online. The organisation plans to make available an online training package for practitioners on e-safety in 2013.
33 Vauxhall Bridge Road
London SW1V 2WG
Tel: 0870 000 3344
www.ceop.police.uk

The Fostering Network
Provides information, support, advice and training to all those involved in foster care, with offices around the UK.
87 Blackfriars Road
London SE1 8HA
Tel: 020 7620 6400
www.fostering.net

Independent Parental Special Educational Advice (IPSEA)
Provides free legally based advice to families who have children with special educational needs, to help them get the right education for their children.
Hunters Court
Debden Road
Saffron Walden CB11 4AA
Advice line: 0800 018 4016
www.ipsea.org.uk

National Care Advisory Service (NCAS)
Leading national body on policy and practice about young people making the transition from care to adult life. You can download the Government's Careleavers' Charter from the website.
3rd Floor, Churchill House
142–146 Old Street

London EC1V 9BW
Tel: 020 7336 4824
www.leavingcare.org

The Place 2 Be

Offers emotional support to children in schools in the form of school-based counselling, and information and advice to both schools and parents.
13/14 Angel Gate
326 City Road
London EC1V 2PT
Tel: 020 7923 5500
www.place2be.org.uk

The Sutton Trust

Carries out research, ranging from early years to university access, and runs summer schools and other projects to improve educational opportunities for young people from non-privileged backgrounds and increase social mobility.
9th Floor, Millbank Tower
21–24 Millbank
London SW1P 4QP
Tel: 020 7802 1660
www.suttontrust.com

Villiers Park Educational Trust

Leads programmes and projects to help able young people reach their full academic potential and develop a passion for learning. It is committed to fair access – enabling students from less advantaged backgrounds to gain places at leading universities.
Royston Road
Foxton
Cambridge CB22 6SE
Tel: 01223 872601
www.villierspark.org.uk

Voice

Works to empower children and young people in care, providing support and advocacy.
320 City Road
London EC1V 2NZ

Tel: 020 7833 5792
Young people's helpline: 0808 800 5792
www.voiceyp.org

The Who Cares? Trust

Provides support, advice and advocacy for children and young people living in care.
Kemp House
152–160 City Road
London EC1V 2NP
Tel: 020 7251 3117
www.thewhocarestrust.org.uk

Useful resources

Corporate Parenting Resource Pack
Produced by the Local Government Association.
www.local.gov.uk/c/document-library

Higher Education Handbook: A care leaver's guide to support
Available from Higher Education Institutions
An annual free guide to care leavers' support at institutions offering
higher education courses across the UK. The guide lists: what outreach
work colleges and universities do, what bursaries and grants are
available and what welfare and accommodation support care leavers
can expect.
www.thewhocarestrust.org.uk/publications.html.

Improving Outcomes for Looked After Children and Care
Leavers, London Borough of Ealing
The London Borough of Ealing runs a programme called Horizons
which provides young people in care and care leavers aged between
11 and 24 with a range of services and support from a one-stop shop
in a youth-friendly setting. Young people are involved in overseeing
the programme. The service includes state-of-the-art premises where
young people can meet others with care experience and where they
can access study support, computers and a quiet place to study,
mentoring, half-term and holiday activities and ongoing emotional and
practical support. The programme encompasses careers advice, health

and housing information and youth activities. By encouraging young people to aim high, the programme has resulted in a range of successful achievements, including 17 per cent of care leavers going to university, compared with the national level of six per cent. www.ofsted.gov.uk/resources/good-practice-resource-improving-outcomes-for-looked-after-children-and-care-leavers-london-borough

In Care, In School
This pack includes a DVD showing scenarios of children in care facing difficult situations in school, together with lesson plans to raise awareness about the school experiences of children in care. Produced by education experts at Bath Spa University and Bath and North-East Somerset Council, working with a group of young people in care. www.incareinschool.com

Resilience and Results: How to improve the emotional and mental well-being of children and young people in your school
A free downloadable guide for head teachers on how to work in partnership with local agencies and to commission and fund additional school-based support for children and young people with emotional and behavioural difficulties, published by the Children and Young People's Mental Health Coalition. www.cypmhc.org.uk/media/common/uploads/Final_pdf.pdf (Accessed 29.11.12)

Support for Young People Aged 21 to 25 with Education and Training, National Care Advisory Service, 2012
Free downloadable guide for young people who have left care. Includes information on the change in the law (from April 2012) meaning that care leavers up to the age of 25 who tell their local authority that they have returned to, or want to return to, education or training, can be supported. Download from http://resources.leavingcare.org/uploads/011f84b4af85da8b047744e2ab0afa84.pdf or order print copies from www.leavingcare.org.

Taking Part: Making out-of-school-hours learning (OSHL) happen for children in care
This pack is designed to assist local authorities, working in partnership with others, in making study support/OSHL an integral part of raising

the achievement of looked-after children, and of good corporate parenting. It is based on the collective experience of pilot authorities taking part in the project and is full of excellent ideas on how to extend OSHL provision to the children and young people in your care. **www.continyou.org.uk/files/taking-part.pdf**

Teachers in the Know

A useful resource for teachers about looked after children, on the Who Cares? Trust website at **www.thewhocarestrust.org.uk/ publications.html.**

Toolkit of ideas for best use of the Pupil Premium

The Sutton Trust, together with the Education Endowment Foundation, has produced a useful toolkit of evidence-based strategies to improve learning. This is aimed at schools to help them make informed choices about how they might use the Pupil Premium to best effect. It also contains information that may be of interest to virtual school heads. Social workers may wish to put some of the suggestions to the child's head teacher.
www.educationendowmentfoundation.org.uk/toolkit

E-safety resources

Fursland E (2011) *Foster Care and Social Networking: A guide for social workers and foster carers*, London: BAAF
This guide examines the challenges and opportunities that the internet and social networking websites can bring to fostered children and those caring for and working with them.

Thinkuknow

An e-safety education website (produced by CEOP, the Child Exploitation and Online Protection Centre) with a wide range of excellent information for parents and carers, children and young people, with short films, quizzes and games for all age groups.
www.thinkuknow.co.uk

Cybermentors

Anti-bullying site where children and young people can get online (or offline) support from trained volunteers called Cybermentors. There is also a programme of support via Cybermentors in schools.
www.cybermentors.org.uk